HOUSE OF COMMONS   SESS

DEFENCE COMMITTEE

Second Report

THE THREAT FROM TERRORISM

Volume I

Report and Proceedings of the Committee

Ordered by The House of Commons *to be printed*
12 December 2001

PUBLISHED BY AUTHORITY OF THE HOUSE OF COMMONS
LONDON – THE STATIONERY OFFICE LIMITED

£10·00

348–I

The Defence Committee

The Defence Committee is appointed to examine on behalf of the House of Commons the expenditure, administration and policy of the Ministry of Defence (and any associated public bodies). Its constitution and powers are set out in House of Commons Standing Order No. 152.

The Committee has a maximum of eleven members, of whom the quorum for any formal proceedings is three. The members of the Committee are appointed by the House and unless discharged remain on the Committee until the next dissolution of Parliament. The present membership of the Committee is as follows:[1]

Mr James Cran, MP (*Conservative, Beverley and Holderness*)[2]
Mr David Crausby MP (*Labour, Bolton North East*)[3]
Mr Bruce George MP (*Labour, Walsall South*)[3]
Mr Mike Hancock CBE MP (*Liberal Democrat, Portsmouth South*)[3]
Mr Gerald Howarth MP (*Conservative, Aldershot*)[3]
Mr Kevan Jones MP (*Labour, North Durham*)[3]
Jim Knight MP (*Labour, South Dorset*)[3]
Patrick Mercer MP (*Conservative, Newark*)[3]
Syd Rapson BEM MP (*Labour, Portsmouth North*)[3]
Mr Frank Roy MP (*Labour, Motherwell and Wishaw*)[3]
Rachel Squire MP (*Labour, Dunfermline West*)[3]

On 18 July 2001, the Committee elected Mr Bruce George as its Chairman.

The Committee has the power to require the submission of written evidence and documents, to examine witnesses, and to make Reports to the House. It has the power to appoint a sub-committee. The Committee or its sub-committee may meet at any time (except when Parliament is prorogued or dissolved) and at any place within the United Kingdom. They may meet concurrently with other committees of either House for the purpose of deliberating, taking evidence or considering draft reports (and with sub-committees for the purpose of deliberating and taking evidence). They may exchange evidence with other committees and sub-committees.

In the footnotes to this Report, references to oral evidence are indicated by 'Q' followed by the question number; references to the written evidence are indicated by 'Ev' followed by a page number.

The Reports and evidence of the Committee are published by The Stationery Office by Order of the House. All publications of the Committee (including press notices) are on the internet at: www.parliament.uk/commons/selcom/defhome.htm.

All correspondence should be addressed to The Clerk of the Defence Committee, Committee Office, House of Commons, London SW1A 0AA. The telephone number for general inquiries is 020 7219 5745; the Committee's e-mail address is defcom@parliament.uk.

---

[1] Dr Julian Lewis MP (*Conservative, New Forest East*) was appointed on 16 July 2001 and discharged on 29 October 2001
[2] Appointed on 29 October 2001
[3] Appointed on 16 July 2001

TABLE OF CONTENTS

Page

SECOND REPORT

The Defence Committee has agreed to the following Report:—

THREAT FROM TERRORISM

SUMMARY

On 11 September 2001 two hijacked planes were flown into the twin towers of the World Trade Center in New York. A third was crashed into the Pentagon in Washington DC. A fourth came down in countryside near Pittsburgh. In terms of both the loss of life and of property this was the most destructive terrorist attack ever. This report examines how those atrocities changed our understanding of the threat from what has been called the 'new terrorism'.

The attacks were perpetrated by al Qaeda, a militant Islamist terrorist group led by Osama bin Laden. There is evidence that al Qaeda has established a presence in some 50 countries. It also has close links with other Islamist terrorist groups. The destruction of al Qaeda and its leadership in Afghanistan will not end the threat from new terrorism.

Another is the scale of the attacks, evidence of a determination to inflict mass casualties on innocent civilians. 11 September was the most appalling example of that—but not the first or only case. There is now a danger that a new benchmark of horror has been set. Other groups may try to meet or exceed the atrocities of 11 September.

There is also an increased risk that terrorists may turn to weapons of mass destruction. We have inquired into the possibility that they might obtain chemical, biological or nuclear or radiological weapons. There is evidence that terrorist organisations, including al Qaeda, have been trying to obtain such materials. We can see no reason to believe that people who are prepared to fly passenger planes into tower blocks would balk at using such weapons. The risk that they will do so cannot be ignored.

Despite the scale and horror of the attacks of 11 September, the United States did not rush into military action. It took steps to comply with international law. It offered the Taliban regime in Afghanistan the chance to expel Osama bin Laden and al Qaeda. We support the measured response taken by the United States and we applaud the British government's actions in standing shoulder to shoulder with them politically and militarily.

The Secretary of State for Defence has decided that the events of 11 September have made it necessary to look again at how we organise our defence. He has described this as a new chapter to the 1998 Strategic Defence Review. This work will continue into the Spring of next year. In our report we have looked at its scope and made some initial observations.

In the past the level of resources put into the defence of the UK has been set principally to reflect the perceived level of threat rather than through an assessment of the weak points in our society. Provisionally we have concluded that in the UK we will have to do more to focus our capabilities on defending our weak points. We will return to this issue in our next inquiry.

The primary responsibility for security in the UK mainland rests with the civil power. The Armed Forces are only used in domestic tasks in support of relevant and legally responsible civil authorities. We recognise the constitutional importance of this doctrine, but we are not convinced that the existing arrangements would be able to cope with a large scale terrorist attack. We believe that a review of the arrangements for the provision of military assistance to the civil power should be part of the further work of the SDR.

The Reserves are an under-used resource in the context of homeland security. We believe that their role should be re-examined. We particularly draw attention to the decision under the original SDR to transfer their anti-chemical, biological and nuclear capability to a regular unit whose principal task is the protection of deployed forces.

But increased protection for the UK is only half the story. Alongside efforts to create a more secure international environment through diplomacy, our Armed Forces will also need the capability to take pre-emptive military action: to attack terrorist groups before they attack us. We will need more forces which can be available at short notice; more forces in other words with the training and skills of the Royal Marine Commandos, the Parachute Regiment and the Special Forces. This issue needs to be addressed with urgency. Our forces are not yet achieving the readiness levels currently required of them.

Additional capabilities will need additional money. The Government should make an early commitment that it will find the extra money to fund any additional capabilities made necessary by this new threat which we all now face.

In conclusion the threat from terrorism is now more pressing and more dangerous. A threshold has been crossed in terms of scale and level of casualties. In response, the global campaign against terrorism must be pursued relentlessly. We must not lose our sense of the urgency and importance of this task in the months ahead. We must not hesitate to take the necessary steps to protect the UK and our interests overseas.

INTRODUCTION

1. On 11 September 2001 two hijacked planes were flown into the twin towers of the World Trade Center in New York. A third was crashed into the Pentagon in Washington DC. A fourth came down in countryside near Pittsburgh. In terms of both the loss of life and of property this was the most destructive terrorist attack ever. Some 4,000 innocent civilians were killed, including some 80 UK citizens. There is little doubt that the perpetrators of these acts were members of the al Qaeda organisation. It has been said that the world changed on that day, that the course of history was knocked onto a different and more dangerous track.

2. In this report we attempt to examine how, as a consequence, our understanding of the threat to UK security and defence interests has changed. We look at how the implications of those events are being addressed by the Ministry of Defence (MoD) and our Armed Forces, and we reach some preliminary conclusions. We will examine some of the issues raised in this report in more detail in our forthcoming inquiry into Defence and Security in the UK following the 11 September terrorist attacks.

3. During the course of our inquiry we took evidence from MoD officials, and from a number of academics and other experts.[4] We also visited the Chemical Defence Establishment, Porton Down (part of the MoD's Defence Science and Technology Laboratory) and held a number of other meetings. We concluded with an evidence session with the Secretary of State for Defence, Mr Geoff Hoon. We also received a number of written memoranda.[5] We are grateful to all those who contributed to the inquiry. We were ably assisted by our specialist advisers, Professor Michael Clarke, Rear Admiral Richard Cobbold, Air Vice-Marshal Professor Tony Mason, Dr Andrew Rathmell and Professor Paul Wilkinson

Terminology

4. We are aware that the proper definition of terrorism has frequently been disputed. Indeed we understand that a failure to agree on a definition of terrorism has been one of the principal factors holding up progress in the United Nations (UN) on the Indian proposal for a convention on global terrorism. For the purposes of this report we have been guided by the definitions of terrorism in UK and US law. Since this report arises out of the attacks of 11 September we have addressed terrorism in its international context, what has been categorised as 'strategic terrorism'.[6] We have focussed on terrorism with militant Islamist roots, particularly as represented by al Qaeda. We have not considered either domestic or Irish terrorism.

5. The definition of terrorism in the Terrorism Act 2000 is complicated but essentially it provides that terrorism is the use, or threat, of action which is violent, damaging or disrupting and is intended to influence the government or intimidate the public and is for the purpose of advancing a political, religious or ideological cause. The Act also proscribed a number of terrorist groups, and actions taken for their benefit are treated under the Act as actions taken for the purposes of terrorism. This definition has not been altered by the Anti-terrorism, Crime and Security Bill currently before Parliament.

6. On 12 October 2001 President Bush signed Executive Order 13224–Blocking Property and Prohibiting Transactions with Persons who Commit, Threaten to Commit or Support Terrorism. In that order terrorism is defined as an activity that—

  i.   involves a violent act or an act dangerous to human life, property, or infrastructure; and
  ii.   appears to be intended—
      a. to intimidate or coerce a civilian population;
      b. to influence the policy of a government by intimidation or coercion; or
      c. to affect the conduct of a government by mass destruction, assassination, kidnapping, or hostage-taking.

[4]For list of witnesses see p xliii
[5]For list of memoranda see p xliv
[6]Q 162

Al Qaeda is proscribed under the UK's Terrorism Act[7] and under the US Executive Order.

11 SEPTEMBER 2001

7. The scale and horror of the attacks on New York and Washington have set in train repercussions and consequences whose effects will be felt for years to come. In this report we can only attempt to reach some initial and, in many cases, provisional conclusions on the most obvious and immediate of these.

8. On 12 September, the North Atlantic Council met and agreed that 'if it is determined that this attack was directed from abroad against the United States, it shall be regarded as an action covered by Article 5 of the Washington Treaty, which states that an armed attack against one or more of the Allies in Europe or North America shall be considered an attack against them all'. This was the first occasion in the more than fifty years of NATO's history on which this article, which lies right at the heart of NATO's historic purpose, was invoked.[8] It was a political act of major significance.

9. On the same day the UN Security Council unanimously adopted Resolution 1368. That Resolution, as well as expressing the Security Council's condemnation of the attacks and its sympathy for the victims, called on 'all states to work together urgently to bring to justice the perpetrators, organisers and sponsors of these terrorist attacks and [stressed] that those responsible for aiding, supporting or harbouring the perpetrators, organisers and sponsors of these attacks will be held accountable.'[9] The UN General Assembly agreed a similar resolution at the same time.[10] The Foreign Secretary described the Security Council Resolution as 'in many ways ... more important' even than NATO's invocation of Article 5.[11]

10. On 28 September the UN Security Council agreed Resolution 1373, which required all states to prevent and suppress terrorist financing and to deny safe haven to those who finance, plan, support or commit terrorist acts. The Resolution also established a Committee of the Council to monitor its implementation. All states were called upon to report to the Committee on the actions which they had taken to implement the Resolution no later than 90 days from the date of its agreement (ie before the end of 2001).[12] Sir Jeremy Greenstock, UK Permanent Representative to the UN, was named Chairman of the new Committee on 4 October.

11. The actions of the UN were the central part of a wider diplomatic effort to develop and maintain a broad international coalition of support for actions against terrorism generally and against al Qaeda and the Taliban regime in Afghanistan in particular. On 4 October, the Foreign Secretary described the extent and breadth of that coalition as 'extraordinary'.[13] It has embraced a large number of muslim states, including Pakistan and Iran. It has seen unprecedented levels of cooperation between the United States and Russia including the latter's approval of over-flight by American planes and the stationing of American troops in Uzbekistan.

12. Some commentators have argued that a significant development arising from the horrific events of 11 September has been a shift in United States foreign policy away from a perceived tendency towards isolationism. Professor Lawrence Freedman, Professor of War Studies, King's College London told us—

> We are hoping, most of us, at the moment that how this has worked out so far will encourage the United States to be much more multilateral in its foreign policy.[14]

---

[7]Through the Terrorism Act 2000 (Proscribed Organisations) (Amendment) Order 2001, S.I. No 1261
[8]The decision to invoke Article 5 was taken on 12 September. For technical reasons, the act of invocation itself took somewhat longer (Q348)
[9]UN Security Council Press Release SC/7143
[10]UN General Assembly Resolution A/RES/56/1
[11]HC Deb, 14 September 2001, c 619
[12]UN Security Council Press Release SC/7156
[13]HC Deb, 4 October 2001, c 691
[14]Q 160

Professor Paul Rogers, Professor of Peace Studies, University of Bradford, however, did not share that opinion—

> I am bound to say that I believe that it is reinforcing the unilateralist perspective [of the United States administration] very strongly.[15]

He argued that since President Bush was experiencing very high levels of domestic support, the security advisers in the administration (whom he characterised as 'hard-core') were able to exert a great deal of influence. This in turn was likely to lead the United States to extend its military campaign against terrorism to other countries.[16]

13. Air Marshal Sir Tim Garden KCB, Visiting Professor, Centre for Defence Studies, King's College London, believed that it was too early to draw definitive conclusions, but he did suggest that one positive effect of 11 September had been on the willingness of the US to engage with other nations, with which it had not been willing to engage before, and indeed the UN.[17] He went on—

> The relationship that has developed between Russia and the United States has been entirely benign and will serve us well into the future. The intelligence sharing that appears to be taking place between nations, including the United States, that was inconceivable before 11 September, may build trust.[18]

14. **In the longer term these re-orientations in the terms of the relationships between some of the major countries and blocs of the world may well have more far-reaching consequences than any military or other actions taken directly against terrorists and terrorist organisations. Already the developments in relations between the United States and Russia appear to have fundamentally altered the terms of the debates on ballistic missile defence and on the future of NATO.** We expect to return to these matters in later inquiries. But for the present, our concern is to consider the nature of the terrorist threat itself. The international community's resolve to deal with terrorism may have hardened to an extent unforeseeable before 11 September, but to what extent has that determination been commensurate with the change in the threat or even in our appreciation of the threat? Do the events of 11 September alert us to the existence of a new breed of terrorist, and does the scale and nature of those attacks warn us to expect attacks using new or unconventional weapons?

NEW TERRORISM?

15. Terrorism is not a recent phenomenon. Its history has been traced back to the *Sicarii* of first century Palestine. Modern authorities have found parallels between current terrorist groups and the Assassins who emerged in eleventh century Persia.[19] Modern terrorism began to emerge in the late eighteenth century. The first reference in the Oxford English Dictionary dates from 1798. During the nineteenth century many of the forms of traditional terrorism, with which we were familiar in the twentieth century, were developed. Between 1880 and 1887 terrorists from Irish-American organisations based in the United States carried out a series of bombings in London and also attacked Glasgow and Liverpool.[20]

16. Even before 11 September a number of writers had raised the question of whether the new world order which followed the end of the Cold War had allowed, or even encouraged, the growth of a new form of terrorism which brought with it a new level of threat. An essay published in 2000 argued '...there really is something new in the modern world... in scientific parlance, the end of the bipolar order has caused the mutation of a host of organisations that used to be purely terrorist groups or purely criminal groups. ...we are now witnessing an almost

---

[15]Q 176
[16]*ibid*
[17]Q 182
[18]*ibid*
[19]See *A History of Terrorism*, by Walter Laqueur.
[20]*The Dynamite War: Irish-American Bombers in Victorian England*, by K.R.M Short, 1979.

biological, uncontrollable and thus far uncontrolled proliferation of dangerous complex entities that are very hard to identify, understand and define within inadequately explored territories or movements.'[21]

17. There is little doubt that the 11 September attacks were the responsibility of the al Qaeda organisation. On 4 October the Prime Minister told the House of Commons—

> Since 11 September, intensive efforts have taken place here and elsewhere to investigate these attacks and to determine who is responsible. Our findings have been shared and coordinated with those of our allies and they are clear. They are: first, that it was Osama bin Laden and the al Qaeda, the terrorist network which he heads, that planned and carried out the atrocities on 11 September; secondly, that Osama bin Laden and the al Qaeda were able to commit these atrocities because of their close alliance with the Taliban regime in Afghanistan, which allows them to operate with impunity in pursuing their terrorist activity.[22]

The Government placed a document in the Library containing as much of the evidence on which it had based its conclusions as it could make public. It supplemented that with a further document on14 November. The second document considerably reinforces the evidence of the first, and includes evidence linking the hijackers to al Qaeda as well as a series of increasingly self-incriminating statements by bin Laden himself. Dr Magnus Ranstorp, of the Centre for the Study of Terrorism and Political Violence, St Andrew's University, who is one of the few specialists on radical Islamic movements and who has written extensively on al Qaeda, told us, 'I have no doubt whatsoever [that the attacks were perpetrated by the al Qaeda network]. There is no other suspect.'[23]

History of al Qaeda

18. Al Qaeda had its origins in the late 1980s in the Mujahedden campaign to expel the Soviet regime from Afghanistan—to purge the muslim nation of communist rule.[24] Osama bin Laden joined that struggle as a member of Maktab and Khidmet lil-mujahidin al-Arab (MaK), an organisation founded by Dr Abdullah Azzam, an influential figure widely regarded as the historical leader of Hamas. Bin Laden was considered to be Azzam's deputy. Azzam was assassinated in 1989, the same year that Soviet forces withdrew from Afghanistan. But the MaK continued its campaign against President Najibullah, the pro-communist leader of the regime left behind by the Soviet withdrawal. Kabul fell to the Mujahedden in April 1992. But the new government, which depended on a rotating presidency between the Mujahedden leaders, was inherently unstable and by 1994 Afghanistan had 'disintegrated into a patchwork of competing groups and shifting alliances'.[25]

19. Throughout their campaign against the Soviet occupation the Mujahedden groups (including MaK) had received substantial financial and military assistance from Arab states and from the United States.

20. It appears to have been the Gulf War of 1991 and its aftermath which turned Osama bin Laden and al Qaeda against the United States. Between 1989 and 1991 bin Laden was based in Afghanistan and Peshawar, Pakistan. He was officially deported from Saudi Arabia in 1992 after he embarked on a campaign against the Saudi royal house for failing to ensure the departure of foreign (ie US) troops after the end of the Gulf War. In 1994 the Saudi government revoked his citizenship. Between 1991 and 1996 bin Laden was based in Khartoum, Sudan. In October 1996 bin Laden issued a *fatwa* declaring a 'jihad' (or holy war) against the United States and Israel and what he called the 'Zionist-Crusader alliance and their collaborators'.

21. Dr Ranstorp told us that 1996 to 1998 were critical years in the development of al Qaeda.

---

[21]*New World Disorder, New Terrorism: New Threats for Europe and the Western World*, by Xavier Raufer in *The Future of Terrorism*, ed. Taylor and Horgan, 2000.
[22]HC Deb, 4 October 2001, c 672
[23]Q 115
[24]This section draws on a Special Report on al Qaeda in Jane's Intelligence Review, August 2001
[25]House of Commons Library Research Paper 01/72 p 42

He explained—

> There has been an escalation since 1996 when he issued his declaration of war, and that has crystallized into a truly multinational enterprise with global tentacles and a global reach.[26]

Before the current military action began, the membership of al Qaeda in Afghanistan had been estimated to be between 3,000 and 5,000. It has been claimed that al Qaeda support and operational cells have been identified in around 50 countries. Al Qaeda also has close links with other terrorist organisations. These include Egyptian Islamic Jihad and other north African Islamic extremist terrorist groups, and a number of other jihadi groups in other countries including the Sudan, Yemen, Somalia, Pakistan and India.[27] As Dr Ranstorp told us—

> We are dealing with a tightly structured organisation at the top. It is also an umbrella organisation. It is less linked along organisational lines but rather [through] individuals within these constituent groups, beneath this umbrella.[28]

22. Al Qaeda's structure and international reach make it unique among terrorist organisations. There is no other group with a comparable multinational component.[29] In August this year Jane's Intelligence Review listed four principal elements that contributed to its strength and resilience. One of those—its base in Afghanistan—no longer applies. But the other three remain, to a greater or lesser extent, valid. Firstly it has become a symbol of resistance against western domination. Bin Laden's pan-Islamic credo draws support from both Arab and non-Arab muslims. In some parts of the Islamic world he is seen as the only leader who can stand up against the United States and its allies. Secondly it has established and maintained links at leadership and operational level with some of the largest and deadliest Middle Eastern and Arab terrorist groups. Bin Laden's own personal relationships with the leadership of these groups and his generosity with funds have helped to cement these links. Thirdly, al Qaeda has managed either directly or through individual sympathisers to infiltrate many international and domestic Islamic non-governmental organisations throughout the world. Thus the al Qaeda infrastructure finds camouflage in the religious and social fabric of muslim communities. There are also two other areas in which it may be seen as qualitatively and fundamentally different from what have been called 'traditional terrorists' of the late twentieth century: its objectives and its method of operation.

23. Professor Freedman told us that, put simply, al Qaeda's objective was to see 'the United States withdraw from the Middle East and ... play no further part in the politics of the Middle East'.[30] Bin Laden is reported to have stated, on 7 October 2001, 'I swear to God that America will not live in peace before peace reigns in Palestine, and before the army of the infidels depart the land of Mohammed'. He has called for the overthrow of those Arab governments which allow US troops on their soil, accusing them of betraying 'true' Islam, and for the establishment of a pan-Islamic Caliphate to unite all the muslim world. He has also claimed to be acting to revenge the deaths of Iraqis, and specifically Iraqi children, caused by the military action of America and its allies and the subsequent international sanctions against that country.[31] The government, in its document on 14 November stated—

> Osama bin Laden and al Qaeda have been engaged in a jihad against the United States and its allies. One of their stated aims is the murder of US citizens and attacks on America's allies.[32]

Since the 11 September attacks bin Laden has also stated 'our enemy is every American male, whether he is directly fighting us or paying taxes.'[33] In various broadcasts and interviews, he has

[26]Q 115
[27]Responsibility for the Terrorist Atrocities in the United States, 11 September 2001, HMG paper, 14 November 2001
[28]Q 108
[29]ibid
[30]Q 146
[31]*Holy War Inc.: Inside the Secret World of Osama bin Laden*, by Peter L. Bergen, 2001, p23
[32]Responsibility for the Terrorist Atrocities in the United States, 11 September 2001, HMG paper, 14 November 2001
[33]ibid

also sought to represent his actions as part of a global struggle between the Islamic and western worlds. Professor Freedman characterised al Qaeda's philosophy as fundamentally 'anti-modernist, anti-secularist' and thus quite different from traditional Arab radicalism and many other Arab terrorist groups.[34]

24. In other words al Qaeda's objectives are not rooted in a particular political context, rather they accrete individual conflicts to bolster a fundamentalist anti-Western credo. Al Qaeda attempts to pull these elements together under what it claims to be a campaign for a political expression of fundamentalist Islamic principles. But its actions are contrary to the tenets of Islam. As the Prime Minister told the House—

> To kill as those terrorists did is utterly foreign to all the teachings of the Koran, and to justify it by saying that such murder of the innocent is doing the will of God is to defame the good name of Islam.[35]

In practice, al Qaeda's objectives are not only grandiose and extreme, but also incoherent and incapable of forming the basis of any rational dialogue. They are non-negotiable.

25. Insofar as there are historic parallels, they are, it has been argued, not with the terrorist groups of the late twentieth century, most of which (like the IRA, ETA, various Latin American groups and many others) had clearly defined political objectives which might in theory provide a basis for negotiation, but rather with the anarchists of the nineteenth century whose purpose was to overthrow the existing order. They believed that they could do this by promoting its disintegration from within through acts of violence and terror. An important distinction even with these anarchist groups, however, is that they were largely acting within the societies which they were seeking to change. The scale of their action and the targets they chose may have been moderated by the desire not to alienate the population at large, and particularly the working classes whose interests they were ostensibly advancing. But al Qaeda has no such concerns. Its operations are directed against what it perceives to be an external enemy. As bin Laden stated in his video of 20 October: 'The battle has been moved inside America ... The bad terror is what America and Israel are practising against our people ... what we are practising is the good terror that will stop them doing what they are doing.'[36]

26. Professor Freedman drew attention to the axiom 'terrorists want people watching, not dead',[37] which had led people to assume that terrorists were not, by and large, interested in causing mass casualties. Rather 'they had clear political aims that required terror, anxiety, a constant background of insecurity, but did not want to create such a political crisis by killing so many people'. But, we were told, this assumption does not apply to al Qaeda. '... these terrorists are not after chaos, they are after death'.[38] Certainly they seem to believe that their objectives can be advanced by inflicting mass casualties. But they also seemed to be fully aware of the potential impact of television coverage of their atrocities. Their record demonstrates a determination to kill large numbers of people—and have the world watching.

27. They do not discriminate between the agents of the powers they oppose (political leaders, members of the armed forces) and the innocent civilians who happen to live in these countries. Bin Laden is reported to have claimed that the killing of muslims in the attacks on the World Trade Center was justified because by choosing to live and work in the United States they had associated themselves with the enemy.

28. The callousness and ruthlessness of this approach is further emphasised by the fact that no warnings have been given for terrorist attacks attributed to al Qaeda. This is powerful additional evidence that while al Qaeda's targets have symbolic importance in political and commercial terms, its intention is also to cause the maximum level of casualties. Neither has there been any subsequent claim of responsibility, although, as the Government have set out, in the case of the

---

[34]Q 149
[35]HC Deb, 8 October 2001, c 812
[36]Responsibility for the Terrorist Atrocities in the United States, 11 September 2001,HMG paper, 14 November 2001.
[37]Q 154
[38]Q 223

11 September attacks there have been clear expressions of support for the attacks and no efforts at denial.

29. Another notable feature of the 11 September attacks was the apparent willingness of the perpetrators to kill themselves as well as their victims. We say 'apparent' only because the subsequent investigations have reportedly thrown up doubts over whether all the hijackers knew that they were to die. The Secretary of State told us, 'There is some evidence... that not all of the terrorists on board those aircraft on 11 September were aware of what the leading elements were going to engage on'.[39] He suggested that the fact that only some of those involved left notes prefiguring their deaths was part of that evidence.[40] Nonetheless, al Qaeda's ability to recruit people willing to give up their lives is striking. And in this case more so because those involved were apparently well-educated and certainly capable of learning the basic skills required to fly a modern passenger jet. In the past, for example in the context of the Palestinian conflict, suicide bombers have been recruited overwhelmingly from the ranks of the ill-educated and dispossessed. A study of terrorism published in 1999 analysed the suicide missions conducted by members of Hizbullah and Hamas. It concluded that 'virtually all the suicide bombers came from poor families, and of these there is a preponderance of candidates who live in refugee camps in miserable conditions.'[41]

30. These characteristics set the perpetrators of the attacks of 11 September apart from what has been described as traditional terrorism, yet the attacks were not entirely without precedent in their conception or execution. In the 1990s there were terrorist attacks on the World Trade Center, US military accommodation at Al-Khoba in Saudi Arabia, US embassies in Nairobi and Dar-es-Salaam, and in 2000 on the US warship USS Cole. There was also a series of bombings in Moscow and one in Volgadonsk between August 1999 and August 2000 which killed several hundred people. The attacks outside Russia were committed by al Qaeda or militant Islamist groups with links to al Qaeda. The Russian attacks were ascribed by the Russian government to Chechen rebels. There is substantial evidence of close links between al Qaeda and Chechen rebel groups.

31. One of the most powerful terrorist links remains that between al Qaeda and the Islamic Movement for Uzbekistan (IMU).[42] The IMU came into existence in 1997, after the defeat of the drug-smuggling warlords in Tajikistan. The IMU quickly became a direct ally of Osama bin Laden and has engaged not only in extensive narcotics trading in Central Asia but is also pledged to terrorist attacks in the cause of militant Islam. The IMU is, in effect, a direct regional branch of al Qaeda, operating for both criminal and terrorist purposes in Uzbekistan, Kyrgyzstan, Tajikistan, Kazakhstan and Southern Russia.[43]

32. So, in terms of organisation, of reach and of ambition, al Qaeda represents a major development in terrorism, but not an entirely new development. '... al Qaeda has taken a long time to develop'.[44] It has drawn on the experiences of other organisations: bin Laden is reported to have described the perpetrators of the 1993 bomb attack on the World Trade Center as 'role models'. Its first major attack on US interests was in 1996. As Professor Freedman told us—

... al Qaeda is a group, which, through the 1990s has attempted to mount a series of attacks. In some cases it succeeded: in a number of cases, thankfully, it failed ... It has tried multiple attacks; it has used suicide bombers. This is its modus operandi, and we can presume it will try again.[45]

[39]Q 288
[40]Q 289
[41]*The New Terrorism* by Walter Laqueur, 1999, p142
[42]See Jane's Intelligence Review, September 2001
[43]For a list of groups affiliated with al Qaeda see *Usama bin Laden's al-Qaida: Profile of a Terrorist Network* by Y Alexander and M Swetman, 2001
[44]Q 108
[45]Q 143

A Continuing Threat?

33. Preventing bin Laden and the al Qaeda network from posing a continuing terrorist threat is one of the immediate objectives of the current campaign against terrorism. This objective is being taken forward not only in the military and diplomatic actions in Afghanistan, but also through a range of international and national measures against the al Qaeda organisation and in particular its sources of finance. The importance of these measures should not be under-estimated. Dr Ranstorp described the modern terrorist as 'part-time terrorist and part-time criminal'.[46] Terrorists finance their activities through the 'triad of criminal enterprise, ...theft, credit card frauds and bank fraud'.[47] He believed that, although the military action had significantly weakened al Qaeda's command and control capacity, many of its component groups or cells 'have been carrying out operations... [at] their own initiative and have received approval for terrorist strikes through very loose coordination with the al Qaeda centre'.[48] The government has confirmed that, based on experience of the way the network has operated in the past, 'other cells, like those that carried out the terrorist attacks on 11 September, must be assumed to exist.'[49] We also do not know, as Professor Freedman reminded us, 'to what extent was anything planned before September 11 to follow on [from those attacks]'.[50]

34. In the longer term the ability of al Qaeda to continue to function as an effective organisation will depend principally on two factors: firstly the continuing availability of a physical base, however limited in size, from which to operate and in which recruits can be trained; and secondly its ability to continue to recruit people prepared to carry out terrorist attacks and to sacrifice their own lives in the process.

35. The military campaign has already substantially reduced if not eliminated any future opportunity for al Qaeda to operate from Afghanistan. There may be other parts of the world from which it could operate, but the closeness of the relationship with the Taliban regime is unlikely to be replicated. UN Security Council Resolution 1373 which required all states to deny terrorists safe haven within their territory should also act as an important incentive on states to act to prevent such bases being established.

36. To tackle the sources of terrorist recruitment, however, will be more difficult. Efforts have been made to reinvigorate the Middle East peace process, so far without success. But, although the Palestinian conflict is one of the most potent issues for al Qaeda, Palestine has not been one of its principal recruiting grounds.

37. Professor Rogers, when he appeared before us on 28 November, argued that the very action being taken against al Qaeda and the Taliban risked increasing support for them in certain parts of the world—

> Over the past few days there have been two occasions, in and around Mazar-i-Sharif, in which large concentrations of Taliban have been killed. About 500 were killed 10 days or so ago when the town fell and between 400 and 800 in the last 72 hours. In the United States that will be seen as an example of responding to the atrocities of 11 September. The use of the AC-130 gunships against the fort in the past two days was remarkably effective and certainly put down the uprising. From the perspective of the several thousands of nephews and cousins of the people killed, who will know much of what happened — it will have been widely covered in the media in South West Asia — the reaction will be different. In other words, what from one perception is seen as a very important step in the defeat of the Taliban, is seen within the wider region as yet another example of something that is almost on a par with the 11 September. We may disagree with that, but that is the perception.[51]

38. The Secretary of State recognised that risk when he listed, as one of the questions to be

---

[46] Q 110
[47] *ibid*
[48] Q 112
[49] Responsibility for the Terrorist Atrocities in the United States, 11 September 2001, HMG paper, 14 November 2001
[50] Q 143
[51] Q 167

addressed in the further work on the SDR, 'How do we avoid the use of force becoming our opponent's own recruiting sergeant?'[52] There is no simple answer, and the question itself should not be used as an argument against any use of force, but it does reinforce the point that the problems we face are much wider than the immediate battle against al Qaeda. The 'new terrorism',[53] which we associate so closely with al Qaeda, would not end with the destruction of al Qaeda.

39. Al Qaeda has links with many other terrorist organisations, as we have noted (paragraphs 21 and 30–31). Whatever action we take to root out al Qaeda, these would continue to present a threat, and possibly, in the light of actions taken against al Qaeda, an increased threat.

40. But there may also be other new groups. Professor Rogers argued that there was—

a generic problem world-wide, which is that there is a range of instabilities that are developing in the global system that suggest that that kind of action [i.e the attacks of 11 September] may become more common in the long-term and not coming specifically from the Middle East.[54]

41. Sir Tim Garden agreed that terrorism could find its roots in injustice but noted 'there is also the Oklahoma bomber and the Aum cult ... in Japan—not a country that is known for the rich and poor problem'.[55] His concern was that a threshold had been crossed—

... now that it has been demonstrated that you can really grab the attention of the world if you kill lots of people, that risk is higher from a range of terrorist organisations or fanatical individuals. Quite small numbers of people can do these things, because some of the means of mass casualties can be carried out with a tiny organisation of perhaps one or two people.[56]

This fear echoes that expressed by the MoD's Policy Director—

One of the concerns I have... is to try to ensure that we have not set some new threshold of horror that other people feel they have to meet; in other words that killing 5,000 people in a major country's major city does not become what other people try to do better than, which leads you into looking at unconventional weapons and a range of dangerous devices.[57]

42. **This is not to say that the battle cannot be won; it can be and it must be. But it will not be won quickly, and it is likely that whatever success is achieved against al Qaeda itself, a number of groups associated with it or sympathetic to its causes will continue to pose a threat.** It is also possible that other groups, not associated with al Qaeda or the causes it supports, will emerge. In the next section we attempt to consider something of the character of that threat.

Nature of the Threat

43. Government ministers have assured Parliament on a number of recent occasions that they have no knowledge of a specific threat to the UK. Lord Rooker, Minister of State in the Home Office, told the House of Lords on 7 November—

The position continues to be that there remains no intelligence of any specific threat to the UK at present.[58]

---

[52]Q 261
[53]Also called 'ultra-terrorism' by researchers at Sandia National Laboratory in the US
[54]Q 166
[55]Q 173
[56]ibid
[57]Q 13
[58]HL Deb, 7 November 2001, c 279

On 19 November, in response to an intervention, Beverley Hughes, the Parliamentary Under-Secretary of State in the Home Office, appeared to confirm that that remained the case.[59] But the absence of intelligence about a specific threat is not the same as the absence of a threat. The government clearly believes that the general level of threat has increased. It has brought forward emergency legislation to take additional powers in order to combat that threat. Amongst these was the power to detain persons, who would ordinarily be deported, but for various reasons cannot be, beyond the time that would reasonably be required for departure. This power required the making of a derogation from Article 5 of the European Convention on Human Rights. Such a derogation can only be made when a public emergency threatens the life of the nation. Moving the third reading of the Anti-terrorism, Crime and Security Bill, the Home Secretary, Mr David Blunkett said—

> Whatever success we can gain in Afghanistan—in freeing the people, in pushing the Taliban, the al Qaeda group and bin Laden back into the mountains—we are still at risk. Those who dismiss that risk, who pretend that because 11 September is 11 weeks ago we can set it aside, are making a grave error.[60]

From these statements we must conclude that, although the government may not have intelligence of a specific threat, they are persuaded that the general level of threat to the UK is substantially greater than it was perceived to be prior to 11 September.

44. Professor Rogers argued, when he appeared before us on 28 November, that al Qaeda was sufficiently sophisticated to have foreseen how the United States would react to the attacks on New York and Washington—

> From their perspective, they will have planned that this kind of eventuality will take place, which lends credence to the idea that probably most of the members of the network are no longer in Afghanistan. It also lends credence to the idea that there is a capability for further attacks. I would have thought that there was very little likelihood of further attacks until now. Over the past two or two-and-a-half months, if they were trying to draw the United States into the region, they were succeeding. Now it is clear that the collapse of the Taliban regime in much of Afghanistan is increasing the rate at which the United States can target the remains of the Taliban and at least elements of the al Qaeda network that are still in Afghanistan. For that reason, I would have thought on balance that further attacks are more likely now and in the coming months.[61]

45. The threat from international terrorism so far, however, has not seemed to be directed against the United Kingdom. The attacks attributed to al Qaeda have been against US interests. In recent years Palestinian terrorism has been largely directed against Israel itself. Algerian terrorists have launched attacks in France. Aum Shinrikyo targeted the Tokyo underground. Anthrax spores have been sent through the US postal system.

46. But it would be naive to take comfort from our relative good fortune to date. In his statements since 11 September, bin Laden has repeatedly issued threats jointly against President Bush and Mr Blair. On 13 October his spokesman reportedly stated—

> Al Qaeda declares that Bush Sr, Bush Jr, Clinton, Blair and Sharon are the arch-criminals... We also ... advise the Muslims in the United States and Britain... not to travel by plane. We also advise them not to live in high-rise buildings and towers.[62]

47. Indeed, in the weeks since 11 September the relative threat to the UK may have increased. The UK is the United States' closest ally and the government have made very public their support for the US and the actions it has taken. **We fully endorse the actions that the Prime Minister and the Leader of the Opposition have taken both to declare and to demonstrate our strong support for the United States. If that support risks making the UK more of a target**

[59]HC Deb, 19 November 2001, c 146
[60]HC Deb, 26 November 2001, c 801
[61]Q 165
[62]Responsibility for the Terrorist Atrocities in the United States, 11 September 2001, HMG paper, 14 November 2001

for the sorts of people who attacked New York and Washington, it is a risk which we must accept. We must take the necessary steps to counter it; but we must not be dissuaded by it from doing the right thing.

48. Terrorism threatens us not only in the UK itself. British interests overseas may also be targetted. Such interests are, for example, British embassies, British owned companies and also British tourists and civilian aircraft. But they will also include our own Armed Forces on deployment and, on some occasions, those whom they are there to protect. It will inevitably be the case that the more our Armed Forces are involved in the sorts of overseas mission for which the changes under the Strategic Defence Review (SDR) are designed to equip them, the more they will risk presenting themselves as targets. Although there have been no recent attacks on UK forces, the attacks on the US armed forces at Al Khoba in Saudi Arabia and on the USS Cole in Yemen in 1996 and 2000 respectively provide compelling evidence of the potential risks.

49. Professor Freedman warned us that 'the victims of our intervention would wish to respond in ways that would make us desist. Either that would involve killing large numbers of our troops or it would involve hurting us at home.'[63] We must be aware that our forces' deployment overseas may lead groups to try to attack the UK itself. **We cannot assume that where conflicts in far away places involve British forces, for whatever reasons, they will necessarily be fought out only where they arise.**

50. **In conclusion, we can see no reason to dissent from the general view of our witnesses, and others with whom we have discussed these issues, that there is a continuing threat to UK interests posed by the existence of organisations or groups whose aim is to inflict mass casualties.** In Sir Tim Garden's words—

> It is a serious potential threat to have the possibility of tens of thousands of people being killed in a single incident in the United Kingdom, this is something that we have not really focussed on before.[64]

In the next section we consider what this desire for mass casualties might mean in terms of the means which the terrorists might seek to use.

Weapons

51. While the attacks of 11 September may have turned a new page in terms of scale and the number of casualties inflicted, it has been argued that they did not do so in terms of the weapons or techniques used. The hijackers' weapons were reportedly nothing more sophisticated than box cutters.[65] Algerian terrorists in 1994 planned to crash an aeroplane into central Paris. Historically al Qaeda's favoured mode of attack has been vehicles packed with explosives. But the attacks also graphically demonstrated the scale of destruction which the unconventional—or unforeseen—use of traditional terrorist techniques can cause. We have been forced to recognise that, in our modern societies, many things may have the potential to be used as weapons of mass effect by terrorists. Not only do hundreds of thousands of people travel everyday in Europe and North America in aeroplanes capable of being used as missiles, but we also transport large quantities of fuel and of toxic chemicals by road and rail. 150,000 people enter the London Underground system every hour.[66] As Professor Freedman told us, '... this attack ... has focussed attention on the things you can do, especially if you do not mind dying in the process, by using much more easily accessed conventional explosives.'[67] He argued that governments must now pay attention to those sorts of vulnerabilities to what he characterised as 'second order mass destruction', 'where you use conventional explosives to generate something much worse.'[68]

52. Nonetheless there has also been much attention since 11 September devoted to the risks from terrorist attacks using unconventional weapons. These fall into two quite different

[63] Q 157
[64] Q 192
[65] Box cutters are knives with razor blades used for cutting open packing cases
[66] London Underground Website: www.thetube.com/content/faq/facts.asp
[67] Q 153
[68] *ibid*

categories.

53. The first are possible attacks on elements of the increasingly complex infrastructure of a modern society—in particular information systems. Much work has been done on the damage which such attacks could cause to financial markets, energy grids or transport systems or even central government. Professor Freedman told us—

> ... one of our temptations is to look at our own societies and think where we are vulnerable and put a lot of effort into areas where, if we were terrorists, we would have another go. So there has been a mass of literature on cyber terrorism, attacking information systems, yet very little evidence that much of this has been attempted on a big scale.[69]

Such threats should not be discounted. But, as well as the lack of evidence of attempts at large scale attacks of this sort, they do not lend themselves to attacks designed to cause large numbers of casualties. As we have seen, the evidence strongly indicates that a determination to kill large numbers of people in a single event is a central element of the new threat. In that context we believe that the role played by any cyber attack is likely to be secondary, designed to exacerbate the effects of the principal attack by such means as disrupting communications or preventing access by emergency services.

54. The second category are attacks using weapons of mass destruction, or of mass effect: in other words chemical, biological, radiological or nuclear weapons. We now consider each of these in turn.

Chemical[70]

55. Chemical weapons have a long history of military use, although they were first used on a large scale in the First World War. Their use was prohibited by the Geneva Protocol of 1925. It did not, however, prohibit their development or stockpiling. They were not used during the Second World War. Since 1945 there have been a small number of documented occasions when they have been used. Most notably Iraq used them during its war with Iran and against its own population in Halabja in 1988, killing around 5,000 people.

56. After a decade of negotiations the United Nations Conference on Disarmament reached agreement on the Chemical Weapons Convention (CWC) in 1992. The Convention entered into force on 29 April 1997, when 65 states had ratified it. By November 2001, 143 states had ratified it. The Convention bans not only the use but also the development, production, stockpiling and transfer of chemical weapons. Chemical weapons are defined in the Convention as all toxic chemicals and their precursors, unless they are intended to be used for purposes not prohibited by the Convention. All chemical weapons must be declared and placed under international surveillance. The weapons themselves and their production facilities must be destroyed within 10 years of the entry into force of the Convention.[71] The largest stockpile of chemical weapons was declared by Russia (some 40,000 tonnes). None of these have yet been destroyed. **Although stockpiles do not have to be destroyed until 2007, while Russia retains its large holdings other countries may feel let off the hook of destroying their own stockpiles. We are concerned also that expertise may proliferate,[72] but our more immediate concern is that the weapons themselves may find their way into the hands of terrorist groups.**

57. There are many types of chemical weapons, from the original blistering (eg mustard gas) or choking (eg phosgene) agents used in the First World War to the more lethal nerve agents (such as sarin which was used in the Tokyo underground attack). There are, however, many other toxic chemicals which could also be used as weapons. As Professor Graham Pearson, former Director, Chemical Defence Establishment, Porton Down and visiting Professor, Department of Peace Studies, University of Bradford, told us—

---

[69] Q 154
[70] This section has benefitted from Postnote No. 167, *Chemical Weapons*, December 2001
[71] *Chemical disarmament: Basic facts:* produced by the Organisation for the Prohibition of Chemical Weapons.
[72] See Q 106 and Q 122

...a trap which some of us can fall into when talking about possible terrorist use is just to think about what we call the traditional chemical warfare agents like mustard or nerve agents.[73]

58. The complexities which this causes are illustrated by the Schedules to the CWC which list the individual chemicals covered by its provisions. Schedule 1 contains chemicals which have been or easily could be used as weapons, and which have only very limited uses for peaceful purposes. Schedule 2 includes those that are precursors, or, in some cases, can be used as weapons, but which have a number of other commercial uses. For example, thiodiglycol is both a mustard gas precursor and an ingredient in water-based inks and dyes. Schedule 3 contains chemicals which are widely used for peaceful purposes, but can also be used as, or used to produce, chemical weapons. Phosgene and hydrogen cyanide are both in Schedule 3. Trade in all these chemicals is controlled under the Convention. Chemicals in Schedules 1 and 2 may only be traded between state parties, but those in Schedule 3 may be exported to any country so long as they are to be used for purposes not prohibited under the Convention.

59. But, however effective the international controls over such chemicals and their trade may be, they may be irrelevant if the chemicals are easily manufactured. We have been told that the science required to produce many chemical weapons is not particularly difficult. It has been described to us as within the competence of a postgraduate student.

60. Nonetheless there are technical problems, particularly in turning toxic chemicals into effective weapons. For many agents large quantities are required. Professor Pearson suggested that 'the quantities you need for an effective attack are of the order of a ton.'[74] Professor Alistair Hay, Professor of Environmental Toxicology, University of Leeds, raised the difficulties of effectively dispersing the agent. He pointed to the Aum Shinrikyo attack in Tokyo where 'they were basically taking the agent around in plastic bags which were then punctured with an umbrella. It did not create an aerosol but just allowed the agent to vaporise.'[75] Consequently it was the people responsible afterwards for clearing up the bags who were most at risk.

Biological[76]

61. Biological weapons spread disease. The diseases are caused by infection with a living micro-organism. In some cases micro-organisms produce toxins, and those toxins produce the illness. Toxins are covered by both the Chemical Weapons Convention and the Biological and Toxin Weapons Convention. We return to this latter convention below.

62. The Royal Society, in a report on biological weapons published in July 2000,[77] identified four main classes of agent—bacteria (causing, for example anthrax, plague or cholera), viruses (Ebola, smallpox, flu), toxins (botulinum, staphylococcus entertoxin B toxins) and Rickettsia/Coxiella (classes of bacteria harboured by lice and other parasites, which might be capable of causing epidemic typhoid or Q fever). Professor Pearson argued that of the three types of weapons of mass destruction 'it is clear that biological weapons present the greatest danger today ... as they are the easiest to acquire, have the weakest regimes and yet have effects comparable to nuclear weapons.'[78]

63. In recent months there have been a spate of incidents in the United States where anthrax spores have been delivered through the postal system. The perpetrator of these attacks has not so far been identified, but there is no reason to link them with either al Qaeda specifically or militant Islamist terrorism more generally.[79] Anthrax is not contagious, but it has been identified as potentially one of the most effective biological warfare agents. In 1970 a World Health

---

[73] Q 105
[74] Q 99
[75] *ibid*
[76] This section has benefitted from Postnote No.166, *Bio-terrorism*, November 2001
[77] *Measures for controlling the threat from biological weapons*, the Royal Society, July 2000.
[78] Ev p 26
[79] See eg Q 117

Organisation expert committee estimated that the release of 50kg of anthrax spores from an aircraft over an urban population of 5 million people could lead to 250,000 casualties, of which 100,000 would die without proper treatment.[80] In 1993 a report by the US Congressional Office of Technology Assessment estimated that the release of 100kg of anthrax aerosol upwind of the Washington DC area could cause at least 130,000 deaths.[81]

64. Practical experience, however, suggests that casualty levels could be much lower. The current anthrax attacks in the US have caused just a handful of deaths. An accident at a Russian military facility in 1979 exposed 15,000 workers at the plant and 50,000 people in the surrounding area to an aerosol of anthrax spores. Just 70 cases of anthrax were reported, resulting in 68 deaths.[82]

65. Contagious agents, and particularly viruses, may, however, pose a substantially greater risk. Although there are effective vaccines against some of those agents, we do not at present have effective treatments against viral diseases once they have taken hold. Furthermore, the spread of an epidemic can be extremely difficult to control, particularly if there is an interval between catching the disease and displaying identifying symptoms.

66. One of the principal reasons why Professor Pearson identified biological agents as the most likely of the weapons of mass destruction to be used by terrorists was the weakness of international controls over the agents. The Biological and Toxin Weapons Convention of 1972 prohibits the development, testing, production and stockpiling of biological weapons. It has been signed by 144 states. But it does not contain any mechanism for verifying that states are complying with its terms. Attempts have been made to agree a verification Protocol. In July 2001 such a protocol seemed all but agreed until the United States rejected it. In November 2001 President Bush proposed a number of alternative measures to strengthen the Convention. These measures focussed on *national* oversight mechanisms and the enactment of national criminal legislation against prohibited biological weapon activities with strong extradition requirements. Professor Pearson described this as 'showing signs of the United States re-engaging and moving forward.'[83]

Nuclear and radiological

67. A terrorist group in possession of nuclear weapons has long been a favourite scenario of thriller writers. It has been argued that the collapse of the Soviet Union at the end of the Cold War has increased the risk of it becoming a reality. The US Central Intelligence Agency (CIA), for example, noted that Russian state-owned defence and nuclear industries remain under pressure to export to earn foreign exchange, and the Agency was 'very concerned about the proliferation implication of such sales'.[84] Since 11 September concerns have also been expressed over the safety of Pakistan's nuclear installations.[85] There have been allegations of links between the Taliban and nuclear scientists in Pakistan.[86]

68. A recent report from the Oxford Research Group argues—

A sophisticated terrorist group should have little difficulty in building a primitive nuclear explosive device using highly enriched uranium. Now, and in the near future, a terrorist group may find it easier to acquire civil plutonium than highly enriched uranium. The amount of plutonium available from civil reprocessing plants will rapidly increase, particularly as more reprocessing capacity becomes available.[87]

---

[80] *Health aspects of chemical and biological weapons*, WHO, 1970
[81] *Proliferation of weapons of mass destruction*, OTA, 1993
[82] *The Svedlovsk anthrax outbreak*, Science, 266, 1202-04, 1994
[83] Q 136
[84] *Report to Congress on the Acquisition of Technology relating to Weapons of Mass Destruction and Advanced Conventional Munitions*, CIA, December 2000
[85] Q 137
[86] Eg BBC news report of 25 October 2001
[87] *Waiting for Terror* by Dr Frank Barnaby, October 2001

Others, however, have argued that the technical obstacles would be substantially greater. The director-general of the International Atomic Energy Agency (IAEA), General Mohamed El Baradei, for example, has stated—

> ... while we cannot exclude the possibility that terrorists could get hold of some nuclear material, it is highly unlikely they could use it to manufacture and successfully detonate a nuclear bomb.[88]

69. But, if a nuclear explosion remains technically beyond the grasp of terrorists, nuclear contamination certainly does not. What is commonly known as a 'dirty' bomb can be made with conventional explosives and an amount of nuclear or radiological material. According to a recent report by the IAEA 'there are currently no comprehensive binding international standards for the physical protection of nuclear material.'[89] Radioactive material is even less protected. Indeed it is widely used in civilian life (eg radiotherapy) and in industry.

70. A 'dirty' bomb would be unlikely to lead to a large scale loss of life. But it could have major psychological and economic consequences. The IAEA illustrates the scale of potential disruption with the case of the accidental contamination of the Brazilian city, Goiâna, in September 1987. A 20-gram capsule of highly radioactive Caesium 137 was stolen from an abandoned radiological clinic. Believing it to be valuable the thieves took it to a junkyard and broke it into pieces. Scrap from the junkyard was delivered around the city. 14 people suffered over-exposure. 249 were contaminated. Four died. More than 110,000 had to be continuously monitored.[90]

71. There is evidence that terrorist organisations, including al Qaeda, have been trying to obtain such materials. A report in the Washington Post of 4 December claimed that US intelligence agencies 'have recently concluded that Osama bin Laden and al Qaeda may have made greater strides than previously thought towards obtaining plans or materials to make a crude radiological weapon'. It quoted US intelligence reports describing a meeting within the last year, at which bin Laden was present, where one of his associates produced a cannister that allegedly contained radioactive material. The report also states that on at least one occasion the White House has cited the increased concern that al Qaeda might have a radiological bomb as a key reason that the Vice President was not available for a face-to-face meeting with visiting foreign officials.

72. Serious radioactive contamination might also be caused by an attack (possibly using a hijacked aircraft) on a nuclear installation.[91]

Likelihood of use

73. There seems little doubt that terrorist organisations could obtain the necessary materials for chemical, biological or radiological weapons. Despite an effective international regime to control the agents required to make chemical weapons, toxic chemicals are widely available. Some states with links with terrorist organisations are believed to have continuing chemical weapons programmes (eg Iraq); in others there are stockpiles which may not be totally secure. Biological agents may be more difficult to obtain or grow, but the international controls over them are weak. Controls over radioactive materials are weak or non-existent.

74. The extent to which terrorist organisations are actively seeking such weapons, however, is less clear. In an assessment of the threat from biological and chemical weapons in 1999 the MoD stated 'so far very few terrorist groups have shown an interest in biological or chemical materials'.[92] Both Professor Pearson and Professor Hay agreed that 'chemical and biological warfare agent attacks by terrorists are less likely than [attacks] through the use of explosives.'[93]

[88]*Calculating the New Global Nuclear Terrorism Threat*, IAEA Press Release, 1 November 2001
[89]*Summary of Report on Protection Against Nuclear Terrorism*, 30 November 2001
[90]*Calculating the New Global Nuclear Terrorism Threat*, IAEA, November 2001
[91]See paragraphs 89–90
[92]*Defending against the threat from biological and chemical weapons*, MoD, July 1999
[93]Q 99

Professor Hay went on to say—

> ... unless groups have expertise or access to expertise in the relevant sciences, it is most likely that they are probably going to use explosives and there is greater expertise around of explosives and availability of materials than there is for either chemical or biological warfare agents... whether it is more likely in general that chemical and biological warfare agents would be used following the attack on the World Trade Center, I do not know.[94]

On the other hand the US Director of the CIA is reported to have said earlier this year that 'terrorist groups are actively searching the internet to acquire information and capabilities for chemical, biological, radiological and even nuclear attacks.'[95]

75. As far as al Qaeda is concerned, Dr Ranstorp drew attention to the inclusion in its 'standard operating manual'—the encyclopaedia of Jihad—of a section on chemical and biological warfare and to 'indications that seemed to suggest that al Qaeda tried to buy laboratories for chemical purposes'.[96] Putting these facts together he concluded that there was 'a clear and present danger'.[97] Later on, however, he agreed that 'even if a group like al Qaeda were to try to move in this direction, they would face formidable technical obstacles.'[98]

76. A terrorist group might decide to use chemical, biological, nuclear or radiological weapons for a number of reasons. Improvements in security measures against more conventional forms of attack might limit its ability to operate and drive it to look for new means. The novelty of the weapons might themselves be an attraction, not least because it would be likely to lead to disproportionate media coverage for such an attack. That coverage would both increase the effectiveness of the attack through the spreading of public fear and also would raise the particular group's own profile.

77. But there are also disadvantages. Such weapons are far less controllable than conventional explosives (or indeed aircraft laden with fuel). As Professor Pearson points out, 'both chemical and biological [weapons] are more uncertain from the point of view of a terrorist because with high explosives you push a button, it happens. You can predict precisely how far the high explosives will cause damage.'[99] The consequences are also unpredictable, both in terms of public reaction (which could include a degree of revulsion far greater than for a conventional explosion which caused many more casualties) and in terms of the action taken against the group by the law enforcement agencies. There are also the dangers to those who have to deal with such materials. Anyone constructing a radiological 'dirty' bomb for example, outside a specialist laboratory setting, would probably receive a fatal dose of radiation themselves. Terrorists may be reluctant to become involved with extremely toxic and dangerous agents.

78. Few of these disadvantages would apply with any force to al Qaeda. And, while on 13 November, Dr Ranstorp was able to say '... there is still no clarity on the exact intent, nor the exact level at which al Qaeda is seeking to develop and acquire [chemical and biological weapons]',[100] there does appear to be some evidence emerging from Afghanistan that al Qaeda has been interested in such weapons.[101] Furthermore, in an interview printed in a Pakistani newspaper in November 2001, bin Laden is reported to have claimed—

> I wish to declare that if America used chemical or nuclear weapons against us, then we may retort with chemical and nuclear weapons. We have the weapons as deterrents.

79. **Although we have seen no evidence that either al Qaeda or other terrorist groups are actively planning to use chemical, biological and radiological weapons, we can see no**

---

[94] *ibid*
[95] Jane's Defence Review, 12 September 2001, p 8
[96] Q 101
[97] *ibid*
[98] Q 103
[99] Q 99
[100] Q 120
[101] eg *The Economist* 24 November 2001, p 22, *The Times* 26 November 2001, p 47

reason to believe that people who are prepared to fly passenger planes into tower blocks would balk at using such weapons. The risk that they will do so cannot be ignored.

UK Response

80. Since 11 September the UK has been at the forefront of the international response. British forces have been involved in the military campaign in Afghanistan from the start. The Secretary of State told us—

> We made a contribution and we continue to make a contribution. That contribution is significant, but I accept secondary to the contribution that the United States can make...[102]

He made particular reference to the RAF's contribution—

> We were able to give enormous support to the strike bombing capabilities that the United States have by offering mid-air refuelling, something that perhaps has not been given sufficient attention. We supported at least 220 of those bombing missions over Afghanistan, at times involving members of Britain's Armed Forces in some very, very dangerous situations.[103]

Our forces have also been involved on the ground and the Royal Navy contributed to the missile strikes at the start of the campaign.

81. The Prime Minister and other senior ministers have been extremely active in maintaining the international coalition. They have expressed their full support for the United States people and administration.

82. But there have been criticisms elsewhere of the actions taken by the United States. Professor Rogers believed that after 11 September the United States might have taken what he called 'the international law route'.[104] This would have involved the creation of a coalition and the participation of regional countries to 'work out ways to bring the network to justice, even though if would take some years'.[105] He was not convinced that the path which the United States had actually taken was the right path.[106]

83. We do not agree. The United States did not rush into military action. It took steps to ensure that its actions complied with international law. As required under Article 51 of the UN Charter it reported to the Security Council that it planned to take measures in the exercise of its right of self-defence. It offered the Taliban regime in Afghanistan the chance to expel those whom they had identified as the perpetrators of the attacks upon them. In the words of Sir Tim Garden 'they waited and they took a very precise and measured response.'[107] On 4 October the Foreign Secretary told the House—

> I cannot emphasize enough that the actions that the United States, we and other partners in the international coalition have in contemplation are entirely within the framework of international law.[108]

---

[102] Q 350
[103] Q 352
[104] Q 215
[105] *ibid*
[106] Q 217
[107] Q 218
[108] HC Deb, 4 October 2001, c 690

84. This is not the occasion to examine the military actions which are still being pursued. We also note that our colleagues on the Foreign Affairs Committee are undertaking an inquiry into the Foreign Policy Aspects of the War against Terrorism. But, we do state now that **we support the measured response taken by the United States and we applaud the British government's action in standing shoulder to shoulder with them politically and militarily.** We welcome the statement of the Secretary of State for Defence—

> I do not believe that in the period since 11 September two countries could have worked more closely together than the United States and the United Kingdom.[109]

85. There is a dilemma for the UK, however, in deciding how it might support the US and most effectively contribute to the fight against terrorism. In a recent speech, Admiral Sir Michael Boyce, the Chief of the Defence Staff (CDS), drew comparisons between the approaches being adopted by the UK and by the US.[110] There has been some discussion about where the campaign against terrorism will venture next, including the possible focus for further US military action, although CDS noted that the current action in Afghanistan has 'had a beneficial effect on the behaviour of potential sponsor states such as Yemen, Sudan and Syria.'

86. He argued that 'The US has less need of consensus than we do, [and] is still seared by their experiences with NATO during the Kosovo conflict'. '[The United States'] current requirement for high tempo operations is likely to put them outside the maximum capability capacity and potential of an institution such as NATO.' The UK, therefore, will have to decide whether it 'follows the US's single-minded aim to finish Osama bin Laden and al Qaeda, and/or to involve ourselves in creating the conditions for nation-building or reconstruction as well'. CDS pointed out that the UK cannot do everything with the resources at its disposal and will have to make choices about what role it fulfills: 'We will have to decide soon whether we make a commitment to a broader campaign—widening the war—or make a longer term commitment to Afghanistan'. A more active role in operations elsewhere will threaten the UK's ability to run concurrent operations. More fundamentally, CDS highlighted the need, as the UK sees it—

> ... to attack the causes, not the symptoms of terrorism. To do this, we need to isolate the terrorist by making it more attractive for his supporters to seek peace. We need to address the hearts and minds of the population, offer effective humanitarian assistance, run efficient information and support operations, gain intelligence, set the framework as we did in Kosovo, and conduct deep operations to strike the terrorist by attritional or other means. We have done much of this already, and are now moving from operations against al Qaeda ... towards a focus on restructuring and reintegrating Afghanistan.[111]

He recognised that as the fight against terrorism moves on beyond Afghanistan, coalitions will change shape with some members hardening their resolve and others 'wobbling', and that we should expect to see the emergence of more fluid 'agile partnerships' which will change their composition as the conflict progresses.

87. We agree that terrorism cannot be defeated by force alone. It feeds on the grievances of exploited and dispossessed people. Tackling global inequalities and injustices must be part of a long term strategy to starve terrorist groups of their support. It is encouraging that agreement has been reached on an interim government for Afghanistan. We note also that our colleagues on the International Development Committee have been examining the humanitarian relief effort in Afghanistan and the surrounding region.

88. The Government's response to the attacks of 11 September has also included steps to increase security in the UK itself. Emergency legislation has been introduced in the form of the Anti-terrorism, Crime and Security Bill. Both the Home Affairs Committee and the Joint Committee on Human Rights have published reports on the wider issues raised. We have

---

[109] Q 363

[110] *UK Strategic Choices following SDR and 11 September,* speech to Royal United Services Institute, 10 December 2001

[111] *ibid*

separately examined those sections of that bill which relate to the Ministry of Defence police (MDP).[112]

89. Practical measures have been taken at airports, at other points of entry and to defend key points in our critical infrastructure. On 14 September the Secretary of State for Defence outlined to the House the steps which the MoD had taken as an immediate precaution—

> Recognising that no specific warning was given of terrorist attacks in the United States, we immediately strengthened the position of key elements of our armed forces. This included reducing the notice to move of military personnel who would assist the police, if necessary, in guarding our airports. Ground-based air defence assets were also placed at a higher state of readiness in case they were required to guard key economic, governmental and strategic assets throughout the UK. Air defence aircraft of the Royal Air Force are constantly at a state of high readiness. Their role is to deter, to deflect and ultimately to destroy any threat from the skies.[113]

The Policy Director told us in early November that 'air defence assets are in place and at readiness to respond to a threat with RAF F3 Tornado fighters and a command and control system is in place to take the necessary decisions'.[114] He did not wish to go into further details in public. These measures are a first line of defence not only for our cities, but also for other places that might become targets. Attention has particularly focussed on the perceived vulnerability of nuclear installations. France has reportedly deployed surface-to-air missiles to protect Europe's largest nuclear waste processing plant at La Hague.[115]

90. These steps against an airborne threat are important, but an easier and more effective attack might be made at ground level. The MDP, during our inquiry into the Anti-terrorism Crime and Security Bill, told us that the extension to their powers under the new legislation will enable them to respond to the changed circumstances of an 'uncertain and heightened threat' by operating further out from the defence estate. Given the increased possibility of suicide attacks, the MDP now believe that if a terrorist reached a military establishment which they are protecting, he would have succeeded—

> Where previously there was a view that we could defend it from the wire and from the gate with some surveillance outside ... now we have to think that a terrorist might launch an unprovoked, unwarned attack from an area some way off the base itself. ... Our activities therefore take us further out ... That means we have to be able to act outside the normal MoD property ...

The example of a hijacked petrol tanker driven by a suicide attacker was given as one of the potential threats the MDP now needs to defend against.[116] Certain civil establishments, of course, are as likely to face a threat of this kind as military ones.

And the MoD has embarked on what the Secretary of State has called 'a new chapter to the Strategic Defence Review.'[117]

THE NEW CHAPTER OF THE STRATEGIC DEFENCE REVIEW

91. Three weeks after the attacks of 11 September the Secretary of State for Defence announced, at the Labour Party Conference—

> As a result of the attacks on the United States, we will be looking again at how we organise

---

[112]First Report, Session 2001–02, *Ministry of Defence Police: Changes in Jurisdiction Proposed Under the Anti-terrorism, Crime and Security Bill 2001*, HC 382
[113]HC Deb, 14 September 2001, c665
[114]Q 60
[115]Jane's Defence Weekly, 14 November 2001
[116]HC 382, Session 2001–02, *op cit*, QQ 2 and 5–7
[117]Q 261

our defence. This will not be a new Strategic Defence Review, but an opportunity—if necessary—to rebalance our existing efforts. We must have: the right concepts, the right levels of forces, and the right capabilities to meet the additional challenges we face from international terrorism conducted on this scale.

In subsequent speeches[118] this work became characterised as a 'new chapter' to the 1998 SDR.

The original SDR

92.   The original Strategic Defence Review (SDR) was launched by the new Labour government in the summer of 1997. Its purpose was described by the then Secretary of State in evidence to our predecessors as being 'to give the Armed Forces of this country a coherent and stable planning basis in the radically changing international and strategic context of the post-Cold War world.'[119] It was set the task of addressing the UK's defence requirements in the period up to 2015.[120] It was explicitly foreign policy led.

93. In the end the review took over a year to complete and the SDR White Paper[121] was published in July 1998. The first chapter of the Review described the 'New Strategic Realities' of the post-Cold War world, and the risks and challenges which the UK faced as a consequence. It concluded that—

> The challenge now is to move from stability based on fear to stability based on the active management of these risks,[122] seeking to prevent conflicts rather than suppress them. This requires an integrated external policy through which we can pursue our interests using all the instruments at our disposal, including diplomatic, developmental and military. We must make sure that the Armed Forces can play as full and effective a part in dealing with these new risks as the old.[123]

In other words the focus of the Review was on the Armed Forces' expeditionary and force projection capabilities. There was also a new emphasis on defence diplomacy and on the use of Armed Forces to support diplomatic efforts to deter or manage crises.

94. The SDR went on to consider the future shape of the Armed Forces. It set benchmarks for the scale of operations which they should be capable of undertaking. It judged that those scales of effort would require only a modest increase in the overall strength of the Regular forces,[124] but they would require re-configuring. At their heart would be 'a pool of powerful and versatile units from all three Services which would be available for operation at short notice':[125] the Joint Rapid Reaction Force, described by the Chief of the Defence Staff as 'very much the jewel in the SDR crown'.[126] Crucial to the effectiveness of this Force would be how it was supported. Much of the rest of the Review addressed the provision of that support in terms of personnel, support structures, and equipment.

95. The then Defence Committee decided 'that its prime task in the first session of its existence would be to shadow the Government's SDR with a view to reporting to the House on its contents soon after it was published'.[127] This it did, holding during its inquiry over twenty evidence sessions, including three with the Secretary of State.

---

[118] eg HC Deb, 4 October 2001, c 809

[119] Eighth Report, Session 1997–98, *The Strategic Defence Review*, HC 138, 1997–98, Q 101

[120] Cm 3999, para 15

[121] Cm 3999

[122] ie dangerous regimes, proliferation of weapons of mass destruction, drugs and organised crime, terrorism, environmental degradation and the vulnerabilities of IT systems

[123] *op cit*, para 10

[124] The Army establishment was increased by 3,300 and the Royal Navy establishment was reduced by 1,400 (*SDR Supporting Essay 6*)

[125] Cm 3999, para 92

[126] Speech to the Royal United Services Institute, 10 December 2001

[127] HC 138, Session 1997–98, *op cit*, para 2

96. Our predecessor's report was published on 10 September 1998. It was a wide-ranging and substantial commentary on the government's work. Having set out the background to the SDR, it went on to examine security policy in a new world order. It then considered the strategy and force structure which that security policy would require and the equipment, personnel and funding which the Armed Forces would need to fulfil their tasks. In its conclusion on security policy, the Committee stated—

> We do, however, have a warning to sound. The SDR may, perhaps, be too led by foreign policy and the commitment to the UK being a force for good in the world. We believe that this focus may have led to a neglect of the level of 'insurance' needed for home defence, and we believe this may need rebalancing.[128]

In its reply the government argued that, despite the Review's emphasis on expeditionary and force projection capabilities, home defence had also been 'considered carefully' and claimed that 'the policy we have adopted reflects our assessment of the current and future strategic environment'.[129] It argued that 'the key aspect of that strategic environment is that the threat of direct conventional military attack on Britain has receded to a degree where the warning time for such an attack can be measured in years.'[130]

97. The Committee also addressed the issue of terrorist threats, particularly from 'state-sponsored terrorists acting on behalf of countries who consider themselves at war with the West but who cannot fight in conventional ways.'[131] It noted the comment of the then US Secretary of State, Madeline Albright, following the bombings of the US embassies in Nairobi and Dar-es-Salaam in August 1998 that 'This is, unfortunately, the war of the future'.[132] The Committee recognised that this was not an issue solely for the MoD or the Armed Forces. Nonetheless, it concluded that it was 'not convinced that the SDR process has initiated ... interdepartmental discussion on how to respond to asymmetric threats on a consistent basis'.[133] In its reply, the Government stated—

> ...we are developing and improving strategies and techniques to respond to them.[134]

98. The SDR was a valuable exercise. It was widely welcomed by the Services themselves and by outside commentators. It provided a coherent framework within which our Armed Forces could be structured. Its implementation should bring real and measurable improvements in capability. But hindsight confirms that, whatever the Review's strengths, it also had weaknesses. Those weaknesses were well expressed by Sir Michael Alexander in his evidence to the Committee in July 1998—

> I think ... that there is a very profound problem underlying the defence posture that emerges from this Review ... That is, we are going to have an extremely elegant and effective defence capability for dealing with a rather well-defined set of contingencies which would involve getting in, doing something fairly rapidly and getting out again. I think that the discontented nations and groups are not [in the future] going to meet in our battle space at all.[135]

The new Chapter

99. In its memorandum of 5 November, the MoD set out its preliminary thoughts on the terms of reference for the 'new chapter' to the SDR—

> The first step is to work through the defence policy consequences of the events of 11

---

[128] *op cit*, paragraph 156

[129] Sixth Special Report, Session 1997–98, *The Strategic Defence Review, Government Response to the Eighth Report from the Defence Committee of Session 1997–98*, HC 1198, para 29

[130] *ibid* para 30

[131] HC 138, Session 1997–98, *op cit*, para 125

[132] *ibid*

[133] HC 138, Session 1997–98, *op cit*, para 67

[134] HC 1198, Session 1997–98, *op cit*, para 32

[135] HC 138, Session 1997–1998, *op cit*, para 126

September, particularly in the areas of defence of the homeland and our capability to counter and deter terrorism abroad. We will also look at the impact of those events on international organisations, including in particular NATO and the EU, and on our regional interests, not least given the need to sustain long term coalitions against international terrorism.

The work will go on to look at defence posture and capabilities, and then take a first look at the implications for force structures. We need to ensure that our concepts, policies and capabilities to deter, dissuade and, as necessary, defeat groups or states which pose us a threat, are optimised to the circumstances in which we now find ourselves. We must do the same in relation to the contribution of the Ministry of Defence and Armed Forces to the security and defence of the UK.[136]

The Secretary of State has warned that 'a sense of proportion and scale' needs to be maintained and that 'we should not encourage the idea that everything has changed, or that everything needs to change'.[137] Nevertheless, when he came before us on 28 November, he set out a long list of questions which the work would need to address—

• Can we base our policy on getting intelligence of specific threats (with occasional misses) or do we have to assess our vulnerabilities to potential terrorist capabilities and counter these?

• How far do we try to defend the homelands (in a collective NATO and European sense) and how should we try to deal with terrorists in their bases or in transit?

• Within the UK, how far should the Armed Forces play an increased role in security? If so, what sort of forces are best suited for these tasks. Should the Reserve forces have a different or enhanced role?

• In the military dimension, is there a role for pre-emption? What is the role of Armed Forces in dealing with problems upstream? What capabilities do we need? What is already clear is that we need fast, integrated operations, involving high levels of military skill, improved intelligence-gathering capability and a deeper understanding of potential opponents.

• How do we engage the causes of terrorism as well as the terrorists themselves? How do we do so on a cross-governmental and coalition basis and what is the role of the military, if any, in this? How do we avoid the use of force becoming our opponent's own recruiting sergeant?

• How do we deter or dissuade states from support or complicity with terrorism, especially in the chemical, biological, radiological and nuclear activities. What if the state has failed?

• What is the nature of asymmetric threats? How does this impact on our approach to operations?[138]

The Secretary of State described this as a 'formidable catalogue of questions'.

100. The Secretary of State did not however, include in his list of questions any reappraisal of the regional or geographical assumptions that were enshrined in the SDR. Yet that document made explicit reference to a working assumption that the focus of UK defence interests would be in Europe, the Mediterranean and the Gulf.[139] Operations further afield would be on the basis of available capabilities and opportunity. The extent and the duration of the operation in Sierra Leone has already indicated that the SDR's regional focus might have to be reconsidered. Even

[136]Ev p 1
[137]*11 September—The New Chapter for the Strategic Defence Review*, Speech by the Secretary of State at King's College London, 5 December 2001
[138]Q 261
[139]Cm 3999, paras 36–41 and Supporting Essay Two, *The Policy Framework*, paras 12–16

more so, the implications of an open-ended war on terrorism—particularly one that will address the problems of collapsing and failed states which create the political space for terror and crime networks to operate[140]—suggest that operations in Central Asia, East Africa, perhaps the Indian sub-continent and elsewhere, will become necessary as part of an integrated political and military strategy to address terrorism and the basis on which it flourishes.

101. As the Secretary of State put it in his speech of 5 December at King's College London, the attack of 11 September—

> ... has demonstrated that we cannot dictate the geographic areas where our interests may be engaged ... in future we may be engaged across a different and potentially wider canvas than we perhaps envisaged even at the time of the Strategic Defence Review'.[141]

Any such widening of the SDR's geographical and regional assumptions, however, is likely to have significant implications for UK force structures, scale of effort benchmarks and the future equipment programme at the very least. **Taken with the terms of reference set out in the MoD's memorandum and the list of questions raised by the Secretary of State, this strikes us as requiring a more fundamental reappraisal of the SDR than is implied by the phrase 'a new chapter'.**

102. On 7 November, the Policy Director speaking of the broad benchmarks for the Armed Forces capabilities set out in the SDR said that, as the work on the additional chapter approached its conclusion, the MoD would work out what tasks they needed to meet, and they would go back to the SDR 'just to check whether that looks right'. He expected that 'we shall find it looks a bit more right than it does at the moment'.[142]

103. Other witnesses also suggested that the conclusions of the original SDR remained valid. Sir Tim Garden told us—

> The SDR is not wrong because of 11 September. All the matters that were generally predicted in the SDR have come to pass. Kosovo happened. We have things happening in Sierra Leone and we did East Timor.[143]

Professor Freedman agreed that the UK was already better placed than the US in the new circumstances because 'there was a bit of this in the Strategic Defence Review already'.[144] The Secretary of State on the other hand thought that it was 'unlikely' that they would conclude 'that all of the capabilities that we have already and have identified are perfectly satisfactory to meet the kinds of threats that the events of 11 September pose'.[145] He expected that they would find that they would have to do more both in terms of attacking the threat wherever it was and of defending the UK homeland.[146]

104. We should also note that we, in the UK, have had many years' experience of dealing with terrorism. For the past thirty years the Armed Forces have been deployed, in support of the civil power, to Northern Ireland. We must not neglect that experience, particularly in the field of intelligence.

105. In early November the MoD told us that, while the exact timetable for the work had not yet been established 'we would expect to be in a position to publish some conclusions in the spring or early summer next year.'[147] On 29 October the Secretary of State told the House 'I would anticipate that we would be ready to publish conclusions in the spring of next year'.[148]

---

[140]Speech by the Secretary of State at King's College London, 5 December 2001
[141]*ibid*
[142]Q 10
[143]Q 169
[144]Q 142
[145]Q 273
[146]Q 297
[147]Ev p 1
[148]HC Deb, 29 October 2001, c 613

The difference is not great, but we did note the Policy Director's response when asked if he would guarantee to keep to the timetable—

> That is Mr Hoon's choice finally ... we are certainly scheduling to be able to publish something by spring/early summer.[149]

We believe that this further work on the SDR addresses a range of fundamental questions to do with our security and defence capabilities. We note the Secretary of State's statement that 'I have set a fairly tight timetable because I do think it is important to conclude this work fairly speedily'.[150] We agree and **we recommend that the MoD makes every effort to keep to the timetable of Spring 2002.**

106. The Secretary of State confirmed that it was his intention to publish an outline, or 'discussion document',[151] in the early part of next year which 'would enable people to react without committing ourselves to anything very specific.'[152] We would welcome such a document and the principle which it embodies of proceeding in as open and inclusive a way as possible. Nonetheless we do have some reservations over the practicality of this approach which we discuss below.

107. The Secretary of State challenged us to provide 'comprehensive answers' to the list of questions which he had set for the further work on the SDR.[153] We will not attempt that, but we will offer some necessarily preliminary thoughts under some of his headings. Earlier sections of the report have already addressed some of the other issues he raised.

(i) INTELLIGENCE VERSUS VULNERABILITY

108. We have not had access to intelligence reports in the course of this inquiry. We can therefore make no sensible comment on their usefulness against specific threats. But there are clearly limitations to what one can expect from intelligence. The Chief of Defence Intelligence told us 'Surprise ... is one of the advantages the terrorist has.'[154] This point was picked up by Sir Tim Garden—

> Even with the best intelligence possible, there will still be the possibility of terrorists succeeding because they have the advantage of surprise.[155]

Following 11 September there was much public criticism particularly of the US intelligence services for failing to identify or prevent the attacks. As early as 15 September some Congressmen were reported to be speaking of 'a failure of American intelligence'.[156] On the other hand the Secretary of State—while understandably giving very little away—did tell us that he was 'aware ... of disruption that occurred to terrorist threats before 11 September because of action that was taken to deal with information about those threats as it arose.'[157] He also assured us that 'a very determined effort [was] being made to make sure that we have the ability to deal with the threats as and when they arise'.[158]

109. Professor Pearson in his memorandum drew attention to a report by the US General Accounting Office of July 2000 which looked at how 'five foreign countries [one of which was the UK] are organised to combat terrorism'.[159] It found that 'because of limited resources, they make funding decisions for programmes to combat terrorism on the basis of the likelihood of

---

[149] Q 37
[150] Q 369
[151] Speech by the Secretary of State at King's College London, 5 December 2001
[152] Q 371
[153] Q 374
[154] Q 13
[155] Q 163
[156] CQ Weekly, 15 September 2001, p 2124
[157] Q 285
[158] Q 286
[159] *Combatting Terrorism: Linking Threats to Strategies and Resources*, GAO, July 2000

terrorist activity actually taking place, not the countries' overall vulnerability to terrorist attacks'. That vulnerability principally rests in those aspects of our modern societies which may be particularly susceptible to terrorist attacks. The report also noted that none of the countries concerned either specifically tracked spending on programmes to combat terrorism or conducted a formal national level threat and risk assessment. Nonetheless, the GAO recommended that such an assessment should be conducted in the US. In November 2001, in a report on Homeland Security,[160] the GAO considered the elements that need to be included in the development of the US's national strategy for homeland security. At the top of their list is 'reduce our vulnerability to threats'.

110. There are inevitably limits on any country's ability to protect itself completely. Indeed, the Secretary of State emphasised the need to have flexible forces configured to be able to deal with many different scenarios and not focussed simply on a few specific possibilities—otherwise we risk inflexibility and planning for the wrong outcomes.[161] **Nevertheless, from the evidence which we have received so far, we conclude, on a provisional basis, that we in the UK will have to do more to focus our capabilities on defending our own weak points, as the GAO advise. We shall return to this issue in our inquiry into Defence and Security in the UK.**

111. In considering vulnerabilities we have focussed on physical points of attack which might be exploited by terrorists. But there is also another dimension to our vulnerability which we have not properly addressed in this report. 11 September demonstrated that we were vulnerable not simply through having lax airport security or the kind of open society which allowed the terrorists not only free entry but also the opportunity to train in the US. Our vulnerability was also demonstrated by the fact that the shock of the attacks was transmitted at great speed throughout a globalised, interconnected system, costing billions of dollars in economic damage through losses caused by instability in certain industries, such as airlines and insurance, and more widely by loss of confidence and loss of growth. The attacks also had significant political, social and psychological effects.

112. Indeed one of the issues which runs through all the questions which have been raised is how to strike the balance between on the one hand informing the public of matters which may directly affect them and about which they may feel that they have a right to know, and on the other hand avoiding unnecessary anxiety or even panic by suggesting that an increased threat of large scale attacks means necessarily that the threat is also immediate. We are also conscious that the act of informing the public itself seems to provoke hoaxers. And they do not only waste the time of the emergency services but also hinder them from responding promptly to real incidents. **But we do not believe that such concerns are sufficient to justify failing to provide balanced and accurate information to the public on this issue. We shall consider how this should best be done in our forthcoming inquiry.**

(ii) HOMELAND DEFENCE VERSUS TERRORISTS IN THEIR BASES

113. The MoD Policy Director told us that, in respect of attacks on the UK itself, the Armed Forces had two distinct roles—

> The first of them is the actual defence of the homeland in the sense that the armed forces have always defended Britain from attack from the sea and in the last century by air and missiles. ... The second thing we do ... is military assistance to the civil authorities ... that is ... where there is not a specific Ministry of Defence responsibility to lead on the subject, but where we support either other Departments or the civil power.[162]

114. There is relatively little about either of these roles in the SDR. Under the 'Peacetime Security' Mission, one of eight identified in the SDR, the MoD stated that 'Support against terrorism of all kinds will remain of the highest priority for the foreseeable future'.[163] But there

---

[160] *Homeland Security: Challenges and Strategies in Addressing short- and long-term national needs*, GAO, November 2001
[161] Speech by the Secretary of State at King's College London, 5 December 2001
[162] Q 60
[163] Cm 3999, para 46

is no further discussion of this role and no indication of how the proposals in the SDR would strengthen the capacity of the Armed Forces to fulfil it. It is clear that at the time of the SDR this support was seen principally in the context of deployments in Northern Ireland and assistance in dealing with attacks in Great Britain by Northern Ireland-based terrorists. The Policy Director argued that it went 'a bit wider than Northern Ireland' and 'encompassed things like aircraft hijacking ... and hostage taking which have been within our purview before'.[164]

115. The risk of attack by air or sea was perceived to be remote, if not negligible. One witness in evidence to our predecessor's inquiry into the SDR wrote 'The only credible direct threat to the UK homeland in the medium term would be from a ballistic missile attack.'[165] In 1999 the MoD stated 'no country of concern currently has ballistic missiles which, launched from its own territory, can threaten the UK,'[166] although it went on to warn that a number of countries were continuing their efforts to develop or acquire longer range missiles. It also noted that some southern members of NATO were already vulnerable and concluded that 'the risks facing Europe are likely to increase in the next decade.[167]

116. One of the premises of the SDR was, in the words of the then Secretary of State, 'In the post Cold War world, we must be prepared to go to the crisis, rather than have the crisis come to us'.[168] Likewise, we need the capability to take the battle against the terrorist threat to wherever that threat comes from. One of the questions which the Secretary of State raised in the context of the work of the SDR was 'how far do we try to defend the homelands, in a collective NATO and European sense and how should we try to deal with terrorists in their bases or in transit?'[169] Later he told us, 'my instincts are to say that actually rather than waiting for the threat to arrive on these shores, we go after it.'[170]

117. As we have discussed, the SDR focussed on giving British forces expeditionary and force protection capabilities. The value of that capability has been illustrated in operations in Macedonia, Sierra Leone and East Timor as well as the current campaign in Afghanistan. Sir Tim Garden told us, 'I do not think that the tasks that the SDR addressed have changed, indeed I believe that they are under-resourced'.[171]

118. We believe that there is no reason to treat this as an 'either/or' question unless it is being addressed in terms of resources. We discuss funding of the additional chapter below. The role of the Armed Forces in homeland defence is the subject of the Secretary of State's next question.

(iii) ROLE OF THE ARMED FORCES IN HOMELAND SECURITY

119. This issue will be one of the main themes of our next inquiry into Defence and Security in the UK. It raises a number of important issues. At this stage we will comment on just two.

120. The Armed Forces have the primary responsibility for countering air- and sea-borne threats to the UK. This is a specific defence task and, as the Policy Director told us, will be 'part of this review ... asking whether there is a longer-term dimension to this which would imply not just making best use of assets we have instantly available, or quick upgrades, but what about the longer term capability'.[172] This is an important issue which we shall return to in our forthcoming inquiry.

121. The primary responsibility for security on the UK mainland, however, rests with the civil power. *British Defence Doctrine*, revised and republished as recently as October 2001, states—

[164]Q 278
[165]HC 138 (Session 1997-98) *Op cit*, Ev, p 22
[166]*Defending against the Threat from Biological and Chemical Weapons*, MoD, July 1999, para 2
[167]*ibid*
[168]Cm 3999, Foreword, para 6
[169]Q 261
[170]Q 290
[171]Q 170
[172]Q 60

... the use of the Armed Forces for domestic purposes is potentially controversial and strict limitations are placed on their domestic employment. The relationship between the Armed Forces and civil authorities in the UK is the subject of aspects of constitutional and administrative law and there has developed, over three hundred years, a legal doctrine governing the domestic use of military personnel. At the core of that doctrine is the absolute primacy of civil authorities; when Armed Forces' personnel are used on domestic tasks they are only employed in support of relevant and legally responsible civil authorities.[173]

There are four categories of assistance that may be provided—

- Military assistance to the civil power: assistance in the direct maintenance of law and order
- Counter drugs operations
- Military aid to other government departments: the response to the foot and mouth epidemic fell into this category
- Military assistance to the civil community: support for the community at large either in emergencies (eg floods) or more routinely.[174]

122. Dr Alice Hills[175] in her memorandum expressed concern that the UK appears to lack a 'strategic focus in our response'[176] to complex terrorist attacks. 'Terrorism', she continues 'can represent an almost military-scale threat that is neither categorically domestic nor foreign'.[177] The Secretary of State thought that this was a fair point and 'one that we need to have regard to.'[178]

123. The Policy Director believed that the existing arrangements by which the military respond to requests from civil authorities provided the necessary clarity. 'There are very clear arrangements', he told us, 'for handover to the military commander at the request of the civil power ... it is that clarity ... which ... allows us to make the best use of our resources, because the armed forces really like to be very clear about their command and control arrangements'.[179]

124. But he also suggested that, given 'the complexity of some of the modern emergencies', the most likely assistance required of the Armed Forces would be in 'reinforcing the command and control capacity.'[180] He pointed, as an example, to the role of the Armed Forces in respect of foot and mouth. **We agree that the Armed Forces have demonstrated their capabilities in this area. But we are concerned that the present arrangements for involving them were devised with civil emergencies in mind. We remain to be convinced that they would prove adequate in the event of a large scale terrorist attack. In particular we are concerned to see clear, accountable and co-ordinated leadership across government departments.**

125. We recognise that important constitutional principles are raised by this issue. We do not have a solution to offer at this stage. **We believe however that a review of the arrangements for the provision of military assistance to the civil power should be included in the further work on the SDR.**

126. The second issue under this heading is the role of the Reserves. Our predecessors in their report on the SDR were critical of the government's proposed reductions in Reserves manpower. They stated 'the Territorial Army are still a valuable resource as long term insurance against the unexpected'.[181] The Committee was also critical of the limited circumstances in which the MoD expected to call out formed units of Reserves in conditions short of general war.[182] In its reply

---

[173]*British Defence Doctrine* (2nd Edition), October 2001, p 6–9
[174]See Ev p 21
[175]Dr Hills is a member of the War Studies Group, King's College, London at the Joint Services Command and Staff College
[176]Ev p 91
[177]*ibid*
[178]Q 317
[179]*ibid*
[180]Q 81
[181]HC 138, Session 1997–98, *op cit,* para 268
[182]*ibid,* para 271

the government stated that it was 'disappointed that the Committee has not been persuaded to abandon its misconception that the Territorial Army can be equated with the United States National Guard.'[183]

127. It would appear that MoD thinking has moved on since then. In the US, the Department of Defense is apparently planning to increase the number of the National Guard's 'Weapons of Mass Destruction Civil Support Teams' from 10 to 32 on the basis of their favourable performance after the 11 September attacks.[184] In discussing what role the Reserves might now play in the UK, the Secretary of State said—

> I have lived in the United States and I have seen the way in which reserves are organised and used there. I think that in recent times, since 11 September, they have performed a magnificent role in reassuring the American public. It may well be that that is something we judge to be necessary.[185]

128. We welcome this openness to reassessing the role of the Reserves.[186] We have no doubt that they are an under-used resource. We particularly draw attention to the decision under the SDR to transfer the anti-nuclear biological chemical weapons (NBC) capability from the Royal Yeomanry to a regular unit. Because of the assessment of the threat from such weapons at the time the principal task of this unit is the protection of Armed Forces deployed overseas. Despite the Policy Director's reservations about exposing the TA to such threats,[187] we believe that there are strong arguments for a NBC capability whose focus would be attacks on and incidents in the UK.

(iv) PRE-EMPTIVE MILITARY ACTION

129. *British Defence Doctrine* notes that 'military activity is about confronting risk and managing it. It is emphatically never about avoiding risk; the military profession is not for those who are risk-averse'.[188] Major-General Milton, Director General Joint Doctrine and Concepts, told us that he was now examining whether doctrinal concepts of 'deep, close and rear' operations of conventional warfighting could be applied to the new circumstances—

> It is a little early to say, but that construct will actually serve us quite well in looking at counter-terrorist operations. The deep operations you can see going out, pre-empting, dealing with people before they have the capacity to mount an attack against you, or perhaps attacking them in transit. We will have a requirement for close operations. We will be dealing with terrorists head on, perhaps back in the UK, but we shall also have this responsibility of looking after the home base and our ability to mount out ... Our instincts in conventional operations and in counter-terrorist operations tell us that the biggest pay-off is deep.[189]

Similarly, in a recent speech, the Secretary of State said that—

> Military doctrine suggests that, in principle, it is often better to seek to engage the enemy at longer range, before the enemy gets the opportunity to mount an attack. This is more effective, and it has a deterrent effect. We must therefore continue to be free to deploy significant forces overseas rapidly. To do this, we must prevent our enemies from tying up

---

[183]HC 1198, Session 1997–98, *op cit*, para 65
[184]Jane's Defence Weekly, 5 December 2001
[185]Q 298
[186]Previous Defence Committees have taken a close interest in the Reserves; see, for example, in addition to the Eighth Report, Session 1997–98, *Strategic Defence Review*, HC 138–I, paragraphs 258–289; Twelfth Report, Session 1994–95, *The Reserve Forces*, HC 65; First Report, Session 1998–99, *The Strategic Defence Review: Territorial Army*, HC 701; Sixth Report, Session 1998–99, *The Reserves Call Out Order 1999 and Progress of Territorial Army Restructuring*, HC 860; Sixth Report, Session 2000–01, *The Strategic Defence Review: The Reserves*, HC 976
[187]Q 81
[188]*op cit*, p 3–4
[189]Q 51

our forces in defence of the home base—otherwise, they have won.[190]

We share the Secretary of State's conviction that tackling threats at a distance, before they develop into more serious threats closer to home, is the more productive approach. Although it fits the doctrine and culture of the British Armed Forces developed over many years, we are not yet convinced that it will be fully robust against sub-state terrorist groups which are not amenable to the leverage of normal diplomatic activity or traditional concepts of deterrence. As the Secretary of State also said, 'we will need to understand better when, where, how and which forms of deterrence, or deterrent action, will be successful'.[191]

130. Whether or not there is in practice a role for military action to pre-empt a possible terrorist attack must depend on the circumstances of individual cases. When we put it to the Secretary of State, he answered—

I think that if there were a sufficiently proximate threat to the United Kingdom and I as Secretary of State could say that this threat was about to affect citizens of the United Kingdom then I would be entitled to defend those citizens by proportionate action that seemed to be appropriate.[192]

The qualifications in that answer demonstrate how difficult it is to answer the question hypothetically: a point which the Secretary of State also made.[193] The question might be better phrased as 'what planning should we do for possible pre-emptive military actions, and what types of action and range of contingencies should that planning address?'

131. There are two dimensions to this. The first is a largely political and legal one. The Secretary of State emphasised 'the importance of international law, and indeed our law, because that governs our own armed forces in the way in which they conduct their activities.'[194] We are by no means confident that Article 51 of the UN charter would provide the necessary cover for *pre-emptive* action. Article 51 applies, 'if an armed attack occurs against a Member of the United Nations'. The United Nations may of course provide the authority for action in a specific Resolution. There may be occasions when assembling the necessary international political support to secure such a resolution before any action is taken is possible. But we suspect that if action is being taken against what the Secretary of State called 'a sufficiently proximate threat', there may not be time. The concept of self-defence in international law, of course, runs wider than either Article 51, or the UN's specific endorsement. **Nonetheless, if the new chapter of the SDR is to propose a capability for pre-emptive military action it must also ensure that such action does not lead our forces to operate outside international law.**

132. In some cases, the Policy Director argued, British forces might be involved in such action at the request of the state concerned.[195] Not all states have total control over all their geographical area. The Policy Director, while recognising that the analogy should not be stretched too far, pointed to British forces' involvement in Sierra Leone.[196] We had previously put such a scenario to Sir Tim Garden. He described it as 'highly unlikely', because terrorist organisations could be expected to seek bases in failed states which 'do not have a government that can make these sort of coherent decisions.'[197] Furthermore, in the case of al Qaeda at least, the international character of its network is likely to make it difficult to demonstrate that specific action in a particular country is either required or sufficient to counter any urgent threat.

133. The second dimension is the form which pre-emptive military action might take. It is likely to involve one or both of two approaches: firstly attack from a distance, through missiles or weapons launched from aircraft or naval vessels, and secondly close quarter action on the

[190]Speech by the Secretary of State at King's College London, 5 December 2001
[191]*ibid*
[192]Q 293
[193]Q 292, Q 294
[194]Q 291
[195]Q 281
[196]*ibid*
[197]Q 213

ground. Professor Freedman told us—

> The British—more than the Americans I think—have understood that in a lot of these conflicts in failed states, weak states, whatever you want to call them, what happens on the ground is critical and the ability to influence what is going on on the ground probably requires your own people there.[198]

We agree. We also note that the Secretary of State in his speech at King's College suggested that 'our armed forces may need to develop a more active role in stop and search missions on land as well as at sea, or in conducting search and destroy raids on key terrorist facilities'.

134. Such actions are likely to be high risk, and the proper planning and training for them will be essential. They also suggest that **we may need more specialist and highly-trained agile forces which can be made available at short notice**; more forces, in other words, with the skills and training of the Royal Marine Commandos or the Parachute Regiment. The Secretary of State endorsed this suggestion and told us that one of his 'preliminary assumptions ... [was] that we are going to have to have more people available at short periods of notice, but there are real implications as to how you do that and the impact on those forces themselves and their families, is something to which we also have to have regard.'[199] Some in the Army perceive that there is a gap opening up between the existing high readiness troops and the rest, who are consequently excluded from front line operational roles. **If interdiction forces are to be an important component of the MoD's response to the threat from terrorism, this issue needs to be tackled with some urgency by the Department; as is highlighted by readiness capability gaps already evident.** The MoD's latest *Performance Report*, for 2000–01, notes for example that only 72% of Army units intended to be rapidly available met this requirement.[200]

135. The possible actions highlighted by the Secretary of State also imply a greater role for special forces. The Secretary of State told us that he would not comment on special forces—

> It is not something which successive governments do, and I am not going to change that today.[201]

We understand that much about the special forces must remain secret and we do not intend to discuss their role in this report. But this does raise an important issue about the way in which the further work on the SDR is to be conducted. Special forces have in the past mainly supported the operational activities of larger, mainstream forces; often going ahead of those forces. **A greater focus on 'interdiction' against terrorist threats, however, could place special forces at the very heart of future operations. In such circumstances, a sensible debate on our military response to terrorism will have to deal more openly and frankly with the size, role and utility of our special forces.** The French Ministry of Defence appears to have made a start, with open discussion of possible changes in the equipment and size of their forces (extra funding will be provided to increase French special forces by 700–900, on top of 2,000 existing personnel.)[202]

Openness and inclusivity

136. We have discussed separately the importance of intelligence in countering the threat from terrorism. At the start of our inquiry the Policy Director told us that one of the elements of the further work on the SDR would be the question of 'specific intelligence against general vulnerability' but that this work would 'obviously have to remain pretty secret'.[203] This was also the first of the questions which the Secretary of State put to us on 28 November. **Taken together with the conclusion which we have drawn that the role and capabilities of the special forces will be another central element in the work on the SDR, this leads us to have**

[198]Q 158
[199]Q 346
[200]Cm 5290, para 26
[201]Q 345
[202]Jane's Defence weekly, 5 December 2001
[203]Q 13

serious doubts over the extent to which the contents of the 'new chapter' can be openly discussed. We await with interest to see how the MoD resolves this issue in the consultation/discussion paper which it plans to publish early next year.

Funding

137. We have been concerned throughout our inquiry that there has been a lack of clarity over how we will pay for the additional responsibilities, roles and capabilities which our Armed Forces may be asked to take on in the aftermath of the 11 September attacks. The Policy Director assured us that in doing the further work on the SDR he was faced with no financial constraints:

> ... we are going to do the work based on what we think is needed and very much at the end ... we shall see what additions might be necessary.[204]

138. Although this might seem encouraging, we must not forget that our starting point is that the necessary resources to implement all the commitments under the original SDR are not yet available. Indeed, the MoD's *Performance Report 2000–01* noted that there remain many areas of capability with weaknesses, with 'manpower and equipment shortages ... the biggest challenges'.[205] And the Chief of Defence Staff recently acknowledged—

> True that expeditionary operations stretch us a lot; true that many of the enablers for SDR have been late in coming and in some cases are still awaited; true that we find ourselves committed to more operations than originally intended; and true that parts of the system have not yet adjusted to new approaches.[206]

Sir Tim Garden described the SDR tasks as 'under-resourced'.[207] He feared that the new chapter would be—for the budget of the Armed Forces as a whole—a zero sum game. When challenged on this, the Secretary of State replied—

> I cannot say precisely what the conclusions of this will be ... We will do the work, we will identify the priorities, we will then have to make judgements as to what are the overriding priorities for the Department within the resource constraints that all Government departments face.[208]

139. We recognise that the Secretary of State is constrained in what he can say. There is a spending review currently underway whose results are expected to be announced in the summer of next year. But there is an urgency to the present situation and a point of principle which we believe justifies an earlier statement. As Sir Tim Garden reminded us, 'the primary role of Government is the protection of its citizens.'[209] We have seen how the attacks of 11 September have both changed our understanding of what that involves and, in the United States at least, demonstrated how a public's confidence in its government's ability to deliver that protection can be challenged. The United States administration has taken prompt action in response and has already made available up to $40 billion in Emergency Supplementary Appropriations, of which $13 billion so far has been committed for Department of Defense measures.[210]

140. We cannot say authoritatively that there are not somewhere one or more capabilities proposed under the original SDR which might now be considered unnecessary. Sir Tim Garden for example suggested that there might not any longer be a need for the British Army to have a significant element of tanks (the Army currently has just over 600 tanks,[211] compared with around 1200 in November 1990).[212] Others have argued that we may not now need as many as 232

---

[204]Q 11
[205]Cm 5290, para 24
[206]Speech at the Royal United Services Institute, 10 December 2001
[207]Q 170
[208]Q 274
[209]Q 189
[210]Congressional Budget Amendments and Supplementals, Financial Year 2002, Estimates 13–23
[211]*Ministry of Defence Performance Report 2000–01*, Cm 5290, p 81
[212]*Statement on the Defence Estimates 1991*, Cm 1559-I, p 33

Eurofighter Typhoons. Sir Tim argued that the UK had traditionally seen a need to keep a 'broad range of capabilities ... a little of everything.'[213]

141. One answer to this dilemma might be to increase the amount of military role-sharing with allies, or perhaps less contentiously 'pooling' of military capabilties. But when we put this to the Secretary of State, while he seemed enthusiastic about the steps taken by some of our allies amongst themselves in this regard,[214] he did not seem to think it was relevant in the same way to the UK—

> ... first and foremost in the United Kingdom we must maintain a range of capabilities that we require ultimately to defend the United Kingdom but [also] to defend its interests and participate where we can in coalitions of the willing around the world.[215]

We do not dissent from that, but **we believe that, if it is to be our policy to maintain such a range of capabilities, it follows that we must be prepared to pay for them. If we are to add a chapter to the SDR, we must add the money to pay for it.** The further work on the SDR is going to run on into the spring or early summer. The results of the spending review are not expected until the summer. **The government should therefore make an early commitment that it will find the necessary extra money to fund those additional capabilities which may be identified as necessary in the light of the attacks of 11 September.**

CONCLUSION

142. This report has been an attempt to look at the landscape after 11 September and to reach some preliminary conclusions on what has changed in respect of the threat from terrorism to the UK and its interests. This is not a threat assessment; we are not in a position to undertake such an exercise. Rather it is a threat characterisation.

143. **Our conclusion is that the threat from terrorism has become more pressing and more dangerous. A threshold has been crossed in terms of scale and level of casualties.** In his speech to the Labour Party Conference the Prime Minister asked 'If they could have murdered not 7,000 but 70,000 does anyone doubt they would have done so and rejoiced in it?'

144. Whatever the outcome of the present action in Afghanistan or the fate of Osama Bin Laden and al Qaeda, we cannot expect to neutralize the new threats easily or quickly. **The campaign against terrorism has been described as three-pronged in that it includes military, diplomatic and humanitarian initiatives. This three-pronged campaign must be pursued both legitimately and relentlessly. We must not lose our sense of the urgency and importance of this task in the months ahead. We must not hesitate to take the necessary steps to protect the UK and our interests overseas.**

145. We shall be watching the MoD's work on its new chapter for the SDR with interest. As with the original SDR, we shall continue to track and monitor its progress. And we shall report on its conclusions.

---

[213] Q 252
[214] Q 360
[215] Q 361

LIST OF CONCLUSIONS AND RECOMMENDATIONS

(a)   In the longer term the re-orientations in the terms of the relationships between some of the major countries and blocs of the world since 11 September may well have more far-reaching consequences than any military or other actions taken directly against terrorists and terrorist organisations. Already the developments in relations between the United States and Russia appear to have fundamentally altered the terms of the debates on ballistic missile defence and on the future of NATO (paragraph 14).

(b)   This is not to say that the battle against global terrorism cannot be won; it can be and it must be. But it will not be won quickly, and it is likely that whatever success is achieved against al Qaeda itself, a number of groups associated with it or sympathetic to its causes will continue to pose a threat (paragraph 42).

(c)   We fully endorse the actions that the Prime Minister and the Leader of the Opposition have taken both to declare and to demonstrate our strong support for the United States. If that support risks making the UK more of a target for the sorts of people who attacked New York and Washington, it is a risk which we must accept. We must take the necessary steps to counter it; but we must not be dissuaded by it from doing the right thing (paragraph 47).

(d)   We cannot assume that where conflicts in far away places involve British forces, for whatever reasons, they will necessarily be fought out only where they arise (paragraph 49).

(e)   In conclusion, we can see no reason to dissent from the general view of our witnesses, and others with whom we have discussed these issues, that there is a continuing threat to UK interests posed by the existence of organisations or groups whose aim is to inflict mass casualties (paragraph 50).

(f)   Although, under the Chemical Weapons Convention, declared stockpiles do not have to be destroyed until 2007, while Russia retains its large holdings other countries may feel let off the hook of destroying their own stockpiles. We are concerned also that expertise may proliferate, but our more immediate concern, is that the weapons themselves may find their way into the hands of terrorist groups (paragraph 56).

(g)   Although we have seen no evidence that either al Qaeda or other terrorist groups are actively planning to use chemical, biological and radiological weapons, we can see no reason to believe that people, who are prepared to fly passenger planes into tower blocks, would balk at using such weapons. The risk that they will do so cannot be ignored (paragraph 79).

(h)   We support the measured response taken by the United States to the attacks of 11 September and we applaud the British government's action in standing shoulder to shoulder with them politically and militarily (paragraph 84).

(i)   Taken with the terms of reference set out in the MoD's memorandum and the list of questions raised by the Secretary of State, the widening of the SDR's geographical and regional assumptions strike us as requiring a more fundamental reappraisal of the SDR than is implied by the phrase 'a new chapter' (paragraph 101).

(j)   We recommend that the MoD makes every effort to keep to the timetable of Spring 2002 for the publication of the new chapter for the SDR (paragraph 105).

(k)   From the evidence which we have received so far we conclude, on a provisional basis, that we in the UK will have to do more to focus our capabilities on defending our own weak points. We shall return to this issue in our inquiry into Defence and Security in the UK (paragraph 110).

(l)   We do not believe that concerns over creating public fear or encouraging hoaxers are sufficient to justify failing to provide balanced and accurate information to the public on this issue. We shall consider how this should best be done in our forthcoming inquiry (paragraph 112).

(m)   We agree that the Armed Forces have demonstrated their capabilities in providing command and control assistance in civil emergencies. But we are concerned that the present arrangements for involving them were devised with civil emergencies in mind. We remain to be convinced that they would prove adequate in the event of a large scale terrorist attack. In particular we are concerned to see clear, accountable and co-ordinated leadership across government departments (paragraph 124).

(n)   We believe that a review of the arrangements for the provision of military assistance to the civil power should be included in the further work on the SDR (paragraph 125).

(o)   We welcome the Government's openness to reassessing the role of the Reserves. We have no doubt that they are an under-used resource. We particularly draw attention to the decision under the SDR to transfer the anti-nuclear biological chemical weapons (NBC) capability from the Royal Yeomanry to a regular unit. Because of the assessment of the threat for such weapons at the time the principal task of this unit is the protection of Armed Forces deployed overseas. Despite the Policy Director's reservations about exposing the TA to such threats, we believe that there are strong arguments for a NBC capability whose focus would be attacks on and incidents in the UK (paragraph 128).

(p)   If the new chapter of the SDR is to propose a capability for pre-emptive military action it must also ensure that such action does not lead our forces to operate outside international law (paragraph 131).

(q)   We may need more specialist and highly-trained agile forces which can be made available at short notice. If interdiction forces are to be an important component of the MoD's response to the threat from terrorism, this issue needs to be tackled with some urgency by the Department; as is highlighted by readiness capability gaps already evident. (Paragraph 134).

(r)   A greater focus on 'interdiction' against terrorist threats could place special forces at the very heart of future operations. In such circumstances, a sensible debate on our military response to terrorism will have to deal more openly and frankly with the size, role and utility on our special forces (paragraph 135).

(s)   Taken together with the conclusion which we have drawn that the role and capabilities of the special forces will be another central element in the work on the SDR, the inclusion of work on the question of 'specific intelligence against general vulnerability' leads us to have serious doubts over the extent to which the contents of the 'new chapter' can be openly discussed. We await with interest to see how the MoD resolves this issue in the consultation/discussion paper which it plans to publish early next year (paragraph 136).

(t)   We believe that, if it is to be our policy to maintain a wide range of capabilities, it follows that we must be prepared to pay for them. If we are to add a chapter to the SDR, we must add the money to pay for it. The government should therefore make an early commitment that it will find the necessary extra money to fund those additional capabilities which may be identified as necessary in the light of the attacks of 11 September (paragraph 141).

(u)   Our conclusion is that the threat from terrorism has become more pressing and
more dangerous. A threshold has been crossed in terms of scale and level of
casualties (paragraph 143).

(v)   The campaign against terrorism has been described as three-pronged in that it
includes military, diplomatic and humanitarian initiatives. This three-pronged
campaign must be pursued both legitimately and relentlessly. We must not lose
our sense of the urgency and importance of this task in the months ahead. We
must not hesitate to take the necessary steps to protect the UK and our interests
overseas (paragraph 144).

PROCEEDINGS OF THE COMMITTEE

WEDNESDAY 12 DECEMBER 2001

Mr Bruce George, in the Chair

Mr James Cran	Patrick Mercer
Mr David Crausby	Syd Rapson
Mr Gerald Howarth	Mr Frank Roy
Mr Mike Hancock	Rachel Squire
Jim Knight	

***

The Committee deliberated.

Draft Report (The Threat from Terrorism), proposed by the Chairman, brought up and read.

Ordered, That the draft Report be read a second time, paragraph by paragraph.

Paragraphs 1 to 145 read and agreed to.

Annex [Summary] agreed to.

Resolved, That the Report be the Second Report of the Committee to the House.

Ordered, That the Chairman do make the Report to the House.

Ordered, That the provisions of Standing Order No. 134 (Select committees (reports)) be applied to the Report.

Ordered, That the Appendices to the Minutes of Evidence taken before the Committee be reported to the House.

Several memoranda were ordered to be reported to the House.

The Committee further deliberated.

***

[Adjourned till Wednesday 19 December at Ten o'clock.

LIST OF WITNESSES (PUBLISHED IN VOLUME II)

WRITTEN EVIDENCE (PUBLISHED IN VOLUME II)

MEMORANDA PUBLISHED WITH THE MINUTES OF EVIDENCE

Page

Memoranda published as Appendices to the Minutes of Evidence

Unprinted Memoranda

Additional memoranda have been received from the following and have been reported to the House, but to save printing costs they have not been printed and copies have been placed in the House of Commons Library where they may be inspected by Members. Other copies are in the Record Office, House of Lords, and are available for public inspection. Requests for inspection should be addressed to the Record Office, House of Lords, London SW1 (020 7219 3074). Hours of inspection are from 9.30am to 5.00pm on Monday to Friday.

Ministry of Defence
Cambridgeshire Campaign for Nuclear Disarmament
Nukewatch

DEFENCE COMMITTEE REPORTS IN THE CURRENT PARLIAMENT

Session 2001–02

FIRST REPORT: *Ministry of Defence Police: Changes in jurisdiction proposed under the Anti-terrorism, Crime and Security Bill 2001*, HC 382, published on 6 December 2001

Printed in the United Kingdom by The Stationery Office Limited
11/2002   792789   19585   CRC supplied

ISBN 0-215-00098-6